-REAL LIFE ENLIGHTENMENT-

Breadcrumbs for The Spiritual Seeker

Author: Aisha Brackett

Copyright Page

Real Life Enlightenment: Breadcrumbs for the Spiritual
Seeker, **Author**: Aisha Brackett

Copyright © 2017

*Editing, Cover and Interior designed by Vivian Gale aka
Freedom Gale* Personal Freedom Publishing,
www.viviangale.com/publishing

Cover Photo by: Shutterstock/**Authors**

Photo by: Asia Hampton

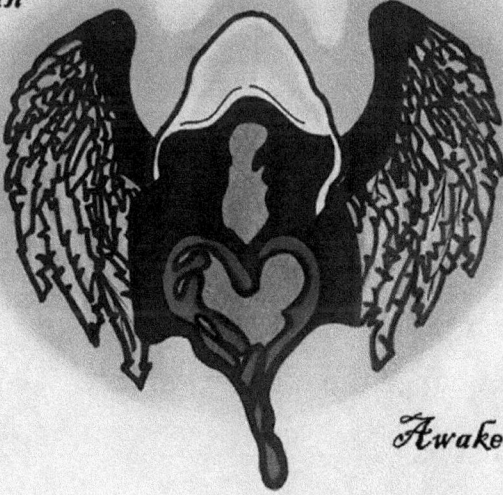
Urban

Awakenings

Contents

Part Three

Foreward

America used to be a society that was considered Christian by majority. People have always sought out deeper understandings of God and the nature of reality, but lately it has some curious souls pulling away from mainstream religion. The term "New Age Religion" has been coined and then beat to death by those who insist on putting God in a box. New age religion is a loose definition of a group of spiritual principles that do not fit in pre-designated boxes. This book, Real Life Enlightenment, is an exploration of some of those boxes from a realistic point of view.

For many years, we have done as we were told and never questioned the rules that had been laid out before us. Now that we are well into the "Age of Information," things are different. We are becoming more curious about consciousness, spirituality, and religion. We also feel a strong inward pull to seek truth outside of what we have been taught.

Some of us have noticed contradictions, confusion, and regret upon examination of self, prompting plenty of inner questioning and doubt. Often, this is the journey to seek the truth. We gather information, read spiritual books and pray...a lot. The journey to the discovery of truths has its ups, downs, curveballs, and wild pitches.

Often there is fear. What will the punishment be in case we are mistaken? Nor does anyone want to feel like they are going against their God. Joining the path of spiritual seekers requires all the bravery, honesty and humility one can muster. These initial questions boiling inside lead us to seeking, to shedding of pre-conceived notions of God, and finally, to a closer oneness with the

Almighty Creator. That oneness, in turn helps each person and mankind as a whole.

The one thing the spiritual path has taught me is the Divine Spirit aka God does not get mad if we have questions. We were put on this "Earth school" to learn and explore. Receiving limited information keeps us more obedient, but at the same time keeps us stagnant in our spiritual growth. Just like with organized religion, when we are on the spiritual path, we must rely on faith that what we seek is right for us and that God/the Universe will give us what we need.

Conscious spirituality offers a spiritual alternative for the misfits, the misunderstood, and the shunned. It gives hope to the souls who are perceived as unlovable and unacceptable by God's standards, according to belief systems. Inexplicably, these same belief systems turn around and in the same breath say, "God is love." We will find out what free will is and why it is such a gift. We will discover our own personal spiritual strengths and gifts and began to explore our purpose for being here on this planet.

Enlightenment is the state of constant inner peace, joy and unconditional love. It is possible to achieve this state in the midst of living in this chaotic modern world. This book is about finding the best avenue for your unique soul. All journeys have similarities, but you have to find what feels right for you. Spirituality cannot be taught. It is a feeling you get when you know in your heart that you are on the right path, and no one can tell you what that is. You have to find out for yourself. There are many different paths to follow on our spiritual journeys but one thing is for certain, "All Roads Lead to God." Because everything came from God. This book is about the journey back home.

Part One

-Step One-

Do me a favor and forget everything you've ever learned about God, yourself, society, and the truth. This is not for forever and is not for the intention of replacing these core beliefs. But if you seek change, you have to have an open mind. This will open you up to the realm of possibilities, which is possibly as infinite as the Creator itself.

You don't have to accept what you have learned as truth if it doesn't feel like the truth to you. It is as simple as that. What an empowering concept! We have the power of freewill; therefore, we have the power of choice. We have choices in all things...including our spiritual outlook. That is our birthright here on this planet. This is what makes us tiny co-creators; after all, we are the offspring of the Consciousness that spawned creation. Choice is the force that propels us back towards the Creator. Without choice there would be no purpose, there would be no need to seek. Without purpose there would be no point of being here. We would have no reason to exist.

This is not to say that what we have learned in the past is wrong, but that there are just more rights that can be explored. Souls exploring other truths concerning God and existence are termed "Seekers." Seekers are people looking for spiritual truths outside of the ones they already know. They have come to terms with the certainty that they have not found all the answers to life's big questions. Seekers make spiritual knowledge a priority and take their relationship with the Almighty Creator as one of the most important aspects in their lives.

Even though you have started seeking it, does not mean you have to give up already established beliefs. The spiritual path is about the evolution of our understanding of God and that is unique to each soul. Seekers can be religious, non-religious, atheist, gay, straight, black, white, rich, poor and so on... We are all here on this planet trying to figure it out so we can live the fullest life possible. Even though the specifics may be different, deep down we have more in common than we think.

In the spirit of this new open-mindedness, now we can tackle hard questions. Is there a God? Why am I here? Why is life so hard? In order to find the answers, you have to be willing to ask the questions.

So, let's play a game. Let's momentarily erase every creation story you've ever heard and interject a radical theory into our consciousness. What if "life" was the result of the Creator wanting to experience itself? Sounds a little out there, I know; however, many spiritual teachings have taught that the consciousness of God has always existed. Then creation began (however they explain it) and evolved, and eventually became what you see on a daily basis.

We live here on planet Earth and while some people believe there is no rhyme or reason to any of this, what if we dabbled with the suggestion that our experiences on Earth serve a purpose? Let's suppose that souls are individual aspects of the Divine Creator that have broken away from a whole to have their own individual experiences. Earth is a "spiritual school," a pit-stop for souls. We choose to come here to learn certain spiritual lessons that this atmosphere is just right for and in order to do that, we are given a body.

We identify with only the body most of the time. The body houses the mind and, as far as we know, that is the extent of our existence. Our bodily functions, thoughts, memories, opinions, and emotions sum up our own personal existence. We think that this is it; what we see and feel is all there is to experience. We don't understand the deeper functions of the mind and spirit. We think we are the body. But in searching for who we are, we, first have to discover who we are not.

Truthfully, we are not the body, the mind, or even the soul. We are the spirit/ soul that enters and animates the body. We are "consciousness" in a body, and we function as individual aspects of creation with the help of our ego. All of the terms will be defined, in detail, a little later.

-The Matrix Has You, Neo-

What is The Matrix? A movie, right? That is what most people would, correctly, say. From a spiritual standpoint, The Matrix uses fantasy to parallel real life. In the movie, Neo somehow knows that he is in a 'reality' that isn't real. At any given moment, he expects to wake up to a truth he can't figure out or explain, but he knows in his gut that there is more to his experience than meets the eye. Spirituality is the same, for it is a thing that cannot be proven, a reality that the five senses cannot explain.

In the movie, Neo meets Morpheus who explains that what he lives in is really a digital construct called the "Matrix." Reality was not real; instead, it was all an illusion. Morpheus asks Neo does he believe in fate? Neo says no, that he doesn't like the idea of not being in control of his own life. Neo seeks the truth and ends up unplugged from the system that used his five senses to keep him blind to the truth. That is what spiritual seekers do: seek how to unplug.

We discover the illusion that was created for us when we discover our power of choice. We don't have to continue to be victims of our circumstances. We have the power to choose. We can choose how we want to feel, not just what we want to do. We don't have to wait until we are dead to have our heaven. We can have our heaven on earth. All we have to do is tap into what is already inside us. That is the power of love, and love is the language of God.

- There Is Nothing to Fear but Fear Itself -

Franklin D. Roosevelt

Love is something we witness all of the time. For example, love creates babies, and babies come to this world full of love. When we look into a newborn baby's innocent face, we are peering directly into pure love. It shows up in family dynamics, romantic relationships, and friendships. We define Love as a strong positive feeling towards someone or something. Compassion, empathy, and sympathy are variations of love. We can actually physically feel this emotion.

Some have described it as warm and tingly. Others say they get a fuzzy feeling. Love makes your heart race and your stomach do flips. We love the feeling of love. We love giving love and receiving love. Showing love is one of the best things we can do. Consciously, we are designed to spread love, and unconsciously, we have the habit of spreading fear. Emotions are contagious. On one side of the spectrum, there is love and most people think hate is on the other but it isn't: It is fear. Fear leads to hate.

Fear motivates us to make a lot of stupid mistakes. Often, we commit these crimes even against ourselves, and most of the time we do it unconsciously. Then we do things like use drugs and drink alcohol to numb the pain that we feel. We call it relieving stress, but the toxins from these 'stress relievers' actually cause more physical stress to the body. Then we must deal with the health problems that can occur in our pursuit to relax.

As we pursue answers to our problems, we usually suffer while trying to relieve our suffering. Our spiritual side motivates us to pray for help and understanding. We put it in God's hands and try not to worry. But then, the thing we prayed about doesn't work out, or tragedy strikes someone we love, and this causes life to spin even more out of control. Uncontrollable events bring along with them more stress and fear in our lives. The reality is we are not in control of anything, which is evident every time we make a decision that goes wrong.

Life can go off the rails at any given time and we are powerless to stop it or prevent it. Every day we become more and more fearful because the truth is when things go wrong, it hurts, and we know that bad things happen to good people all the time.

The collective consciousness of the human race is a fickle thing. As we change and evolve, so do our standards of what is acceptable. We all make mistakes and have struggled on some level with parts of our life, but the desire for acceptance propels us to cover up things we feel others would not like or accept. Honesty would help us avoid a lot of unnecessary mental pain, but the ego is easily damaged.

We spend a lot of time living in the past and not accepting what is. We spend a lot of mental time in the future as well, almost never fully engrossed in the present moment. We also ride this sick merry go round of trying to control our life only to watch it go out of control at any given time. We hope, we pray, we wish for good and then bad happens. This cycle is stressful as hell.

Tragedies seem to happen without warning and it seems like all of prayers go unanswered. Some? Yes. All? No. We try to have faith, but emotions and events sometimes shake our faith to the very core of our being. Life moves so fast sometimes that we barely get enough time to catch our breath.

We also have a habit of putting the information we receive into categorical boxes in our brains. Our opinions of right and wrong, good and bad, lead to judgment and judgmental behavior leads to conflict. This natural instinct contradicts acceptance and things we were taught like, "The Golden Rule," which says to treat people the way you want to be treated!

Categorizing information is a primal instinct that was very useful ages ago when we lived alongside the threat of danger. It was what is called, "the fight or flight" response. Long ago, we had to remember which path to hunt and which path to avoid. We had to remember the geographical location of something that could put us in danger. Even though we don't need to gear our body up to flee from possible harm anymore, the instinct is still there. It shows up as anxiety and stress.

Stress is the result of witnessing something we have put into our little brain box as "wrong." This inner alarm signals to us the potential for suffering which we try to avoid because, frankly, it just doesn't feel good. In these moments where we need to protect ourselves, or figure things out, or change a situation, that natural instinct to LOVE goes right out of the window. We are in survival mode.

An example of love gone astray would be marriage as the institution it is today. It is supposed to be an example of love, but if you look closer you can see everything that is wrong with the world when two people partner in a marriage. We already see ourselves as imperfect creatures that need to be improved on. So, we try to work on our imperfections.

Our desire for companionship is a natural occurrence imbedded in us to ensure that our species doesn't die out. Since some of our spirits have been fragmented due to childhood traumas, we end up as adults with splintered souls. These incomplete humans, at times, seek out other human beings that are incomplete in their own ways and expect their partner to make them complete. Two shattered souls do not a complete soul make.

When we realize this - not only can that other person not make us happy - but what we expected that went along with marriage really just brought us more stress and pain, our marriages fail. Even worse, humans often have this crazy magnetism for attracting their opposite. We are still figuring out how to be happy, and now we have saddled ourselves with the job of making someone else happy when we can't even make ourselves happy. That sounds like a scenario with the potential for failure.

The key to finding peace and happiness within yourself is to accept every part of you: the good, the bad, the ugly, the incomplete, the pained, and the fragmented. You need to be honest with yourself. You have to go through the storm to get to the sunshine. Every part of you is perfect and purposeful even if it doesn't look like it. You have to learn how to accept every event as one that was destined to be. If it wasn't meant to be it, it wouldn't have happened.

Every minute has purpose and the potential to teach a lesson. We have to just trust that the Celestial Soul Maker a.k.a. God did not make a mistake when creating our existence or determining our lives paths.

There is nothing to fear but fear itself. Fear is an illusion: It is not real. We feed into the illusion, and it becomes reality. Our challenge is to become more of aware of ourselves, how we react to things and why we react the way we react. After we become conscious of the behavior, only then, can we change it. You cannot fix a problem that you are not aware of.

-So, Who Are You? -

When we think of the traditional definition of ego, we often think about characteristics of arrogance and conceit, but the spiritual definition has a different spin. Ego is identified as our sense of self. It gives us our individuality. It houses thoughts, concepts, beliefs, conditioning, and emotions. Upon birth of the body, there is also the birth of the ego.

What is the ego? For starters, it is who you think you are because it is who you have been for so long. Ego is self-image and self-projection controlled by the body, the brain, and the emotions. It is formed through conditioning and begins to develop at birth. We will get into what exactly "conditioning" is a little later. Ego is the small "i". It is the sense of self that gets developed over time that we view as separate from everything else.

Deep down, each person has a spirit/soul that is immortal, eternal, and infinite. The ego only lasts as long as this particular body does. Its purpose is to give us a sense of individual self and provide protection against physical, mental, emotional, and spiritual trauma that would damage our inner spirits/souls before they had time to fully develop. The ego protects our human psyche.

The human psyche is very fragile and easily buckles and breaks under pressure. As ego develops and strengthens, it acts as the protector of the soul/ spirit complex. With every traumatic experience we suffer, the ego adds a layer to itself for further protection. This pulls us further and further away from our spirit. We end up in a state of complete unconsciousness. Being unconscious means being stuck in our same cycles of bad habits without having the strength, knowledge, and willpower to break them.

We are born as true awareness, but since we forget everything prior to birth, the ego serves on the front line in our army of intelligent existence. We begin to identify with our ego instead of using it as the tool it was meant to be. We think it *is* us; however, it's really just the covering, the pale patina of the spirit. Underneath the rough charcoal covering our spirit shines bright as a diamond. 95% of our energy is spent protecting, defending, and maintaining the ego. We use so much energy doing that, we rarely get to live without it.

The ego acts like it is tough, but it isn't. Its bark is far worse than its bite. It tries to shield our spirits from mental pain, but the trauma still seeps in. So, what it does is deflect all negativity away from the inner core. Any unwanted feelings or bad experiences get buried or rejected. That act of burying them actually sends them directly to our spirit because it resides in the subconscious with our memories.

The ego isn't the mind, it is an aspect of the mind. The makings of the ego, its roots, and origins, are stored in the subconscious mind. After a while, we just react to things in our lives out of habit. We don't even have to think about it. This is why change is hard for the human mind to accomplish. Who we *think* we are, becomes autonomic after a while.

Our ego's opinions are based on our individual experiences, DNA and genetics, image projections, self-image, beliefs and preconceived notions. What is real and possible is based on what we see around us, and what we have learned and experienced in the past. Also, the ego works hard to present the most perfect version of ourselves because we don't want to be judged. It thrives on our need for acceptance. Ego tells you who you are based on your status, profession, talents, possession, and titles and it tries to convince you wholeheartedly that these accomplishments are who you are. Your ego lies to you.

Ego is necessary, however, because it feeds and develops areas of our individual personalities that motivate creation. It builds self-confidence to accomplish goals that provide purpose. There can be no blockbuster movie, accomplished artist, or successful singer without ego creating a belief that the success could be achieved in the first place.

-*Egomaniac*-

The ego is a separate entity from our true nature and we have the ability to control it and keep it in check. The ego and the spirit are two separate energies. The ego is the "carnal" man and what some religious teachings refer to as having been born into sin. *The spirit or the spiritual man is what is known as the part of us that created in the image of God.*

We strive for perfection in the eyes of our God, and we all know how hard this is. The ego is the reason why it is so hard. We watch thoughts arise in our mind and feed them with our emotions. Thoughts and emotions are planted in ego's garden as it collects experiences, categorizes thoughts and opinions, and formulates beliefs. It almost always goes overboard with its duties.

We have energy centers in the body that are vehicles for the ego's and the spirit's energies according to a multitude of various spiritual teachings. There are seven main energy centers called Chakras. The three lower chakras are all about the ego's energy. The fourth chakra, called the heart chakra, focuses on love and is the bridge to the three higher chakras. When they're open and developed, they lead us away from selfish and egotistical thinking and towards more important matters of the spirit. We connect to the true image of God, meaning we now live in love, spirit, and truth.

The first step to calming the wild-natured ego is to look at it and accept it for what it is and what it does. It has a purpose. It gives us a sense of identity. We need to calm it because it causes unnecessary pain and suffering. It helps solidify a false sense of separation from the Almighty Creator and from each other.

We are not separate, however, in all honesty; this is an illusion. There is a duality to every human, ego and spirit. The ego is housed in our bodies and is just as limited as our bodies. That which watches the ego, participates with the ego and even conquers and tames the ego is infinite.

The first stages of ego development come with early childhood development. We identified with our emotions as toddlers and really, that's all there was to us: happy, sad, angry, excited or scared. There is no rationality, just raw feelings. We do not know or learn that emotions are tools. We begin to make decisions based on these emotions and develop individual identities of self. The funny part is we spend the rest of our lives doing this.

During adolescence and our young adult years, self-esteem develops. This is also ego development. We look to our peers to decide what is and is not acceptable. We are still at the stage of developing individual identities. We want everyone to like us because it makes us feel better about ourselves. We still react on the impulses of our emotions wholeheartedly.

It's common knowledge that teenagers are moody and difficult to deal with. As children, our thoughts were guided by our parents, but as teenagers, our ego was fed enough experiences that it now feels strong or wise enough to make life decisions. Or at least it thinks it can. We all know how that usually ends.

We grow into adulthood making decisions and dealing with the consequences of those decisions. Ego has grown strong now and has a mind of its own. This leads to many mistakes....a shit load of them. With maturity, we lose the urge to act completely on impulse. We become self-aware of our personal choices and the consequences that comes with them.

Becoming self-conscious is a painful process because when we begin to weigh the outcomes of our choices, we often look outside of ourselves for guidance. We use other people as models for living, compasses for life's journey and even moral rulers. To us, they look like they have it all together. We see confidence, maturity, and success in their lives and it reflects back to us everything we are not.

Some people do not believe or are not aware that on the inside, everyone goes through the same unsureness and self-doubt. We parrot certain traits that we see the majority of people do. We watch our peers, friends, family, and society sets the precedence regarding what is to be accomplished in our own lives.

The phrase, "Keeping up with the Jones," describes what happens next. We compete, subliminally, with each other to have the most and the best possessions. We are trying to buy happiness. Does it work? Sometimes. Each time that temporary euphoria wears off, a material item has to be purchased again, thus keeping this cycle of seeking outside ourselves alive and well. We'll be happy momentarily and in debt most of the time.

At one point in time, I was obsessed with buying shoes. It was how I dealt with life's losses. Going through a breakup? Buy a pair of shoes. Hard day at work? Buy a pair of shoes. After a while, I had a very extensive shoe collection. Yeah, my feet looked really cute but I realized I wasn't solving any of my problems; I was only pacifying myself.

In modern society, group consciousness is favored over free thinking. Usually, we think what the majority thinks. That's just how it is. And because we fear what we don't understand, non-traditional thinking is discouraged. Society teaches that success is measured in terms of acceptance, accomplishments, prestige, fame, and money. Even though the word "self-esteem" contains the word "self;"

its development is based on other people's opinions of us more often than our opinions of ourselves.

Self-esteem being, how one feels about oneself, is formed by outside influences from birth through death. Teenagers struggle to find a sense of identity and acceptance by peers and this carries over into adulthood. We compete with each other to have the best houses, cars, clothes, families, and careers. Group consciousness is something that is common, especially in the Western world. It is, essentially, the "go along with the herd" mentality, doing what everybody else is doing, not ruffling any feathers.

Most of the time this behavior is unconscious. Radical behavior is shunned and ostracized. Moving from a religious background to an unstructured belief system was very difficult for me. Family, friends, and peers were quick to express their objections without trying to seek an understanding of why I incorporated new beliefs into my spiritual regimen. It was a very lonely feeling.

When we want to feel accepted, it is quite natural to look to our fellow man for confirmation and inspiration. We want to make sure that we are doing it right. The praise and approval we get in turn gives our false sense of self a convincing argument of wholeness and well-being. Any negative feedback can create emotional scars that penetrate the ego and are etched right onto the soul.

The ego looks like a good guard dog, but burglars slip past all the time and invade our peace. Our survival instinct gave birth to the ego for protection for our souls. The outer shell of protection can easily be penetrated given the right situation, and there is nothing we can do to avoid this. Suffering losses and experiencing mental pain is simply a part of the human experience.

-Ego Extensions-

We have to know what is going on with ourselves first before we can change it. Most people assume they are their bodies, that they are their feelings and their five senses and that is it. This notion originates in the first chakra. Our autonomic instincts are pre-programmed in our minds. There is a saying, "Self-preservation is the first rule." This means we are born with survival instincts that kick in when needed. For example, if a six-month-old baby is thrown face down in the water their instinct is to flip over and use their arms and legs to keep them afloat.

The need for food and shelter drives us to do what we have to do to survive. Sex/procreation is another pre-programmed instinct and it ensures the survival of all species. When we spend all our energy feeding the lower instincts we often wind up miserable because we are out of balance with our very being. But since we don't exactly know what our true nature is, getting ourselves back in balance is no easy feat.

Most of the time, we just keep feeding the need to survive which supports the drive for material possessions to keep the body comfortable. We think that if the body is kept comfortable that we will maintain happiness. Material possessions do bring happiness to some but are fleeting and fickle. No matter how much one wants to pretend that they are content, the desire for more will always be insatiable. We can say, I have careers, houses, kids, and cars and think we are successful according to society's standards, right? So, that's it. We're supposed to be happy, right? Then, why are we so damn miserable?

When you believe that you are the body, you live in constant deep-seated fear, because the body is only temporary. There we go dealing with that "fear issue," again.

We are constantly reminded of our mortality and it creates a deep-seated, unconscious fear. The key word in that phrase is *unconscious* we aren't even aware that fear is there.

When we look at each other we don't see souls, we don't see spirit animating the body. We see bodies. We use our five senses to make sense of what is going on around us. When death comes along it really looks personal. Like, one minute the five senses are in use, the next minute, we are a fucking memory. No matter how the body is cared for, and disposed of, that person will forever more be a memory.

The average person cannot peer into the spirit world and NO ONE knows for certain what happens after death. Death is the ultimate known and unknown, the ultimate certainty and uncertainty.

Death will come no matter what you do, who you are, and how much money you have. That body that you have inhabited for years will one day cease to exist. You have groomed this body, agonized over its changing shape, adorned it with beautiful clothing, jewelry, sweet smelling scents, and you have grown attached to it. One day it will be gone. We run from that fact, ignore that fact and pretend like it doesn't exist but yet, it still terrifies us that death is so permanent.

You have some people who carefully choose what they put in their bodies; they exercise and get rest so they can live as long as they can. You have people, on the other hand, who have a "Y.O.L.O.," (you only live once) type of attitude. They smoke, drink, party, have fun and make reckless decisions. They know that the body is temporary, and they act like they don't care but this behavior is still a front. They are just as scared as the next person. Drugs and alcohol are numbing agents to deal with life, to deal with stress....and to deal with death.

There are people who refuse to become organ donors. It seems like a non-factor, right? I mean you're gone, but the attachment to the body is so extreme that some people refuse to relinquish ownership of their organs to someone else. Those organs are possessions. To them, they are their bodies and all its contents. We think that when body is gone, we are gone because that is all we are.

When you look in the mirror what do you see? You see yourself. Rarely does one look in the mirror and say, "I see spirit experiencing creation that is created by spirit," even though that is a more accurate assessment.

The self-identification with the body formulates the "I" and everything else in our personal life is an extension of that "I." The extensions of ego make up who you are, where you were born, who your family is and so on. The extensions of the ego are the roles we play while we are here on this planet. We play the roles of gender, parent, child, family member, spouse, occupation and so on. But the gag is: we identify the roles we play as if they are us! We feed into these roles. That is why our lives are so stressful and hard. We identify with the "I." We feed into the "I." This is where the emotions get attached. This is where things become hard to let go of. Ego is controlling the game and we are pawns of it.

The brain chooses right or wrong based on of cataloged opinions and beliefs, and emotions process the situations for us. Most of us get caught up in the emotional part. Physical sensations accompany emotions, which make them even more tangible. Adrenaline races through our bloodstream causing our hearts to beat fast. We feel flushed, hot to the touch, our hands tremble, we feel queasy, and we even cry. Emotions attach the soul to the body like suction cups. This cements the false impression that we are only the body. We end up having a lot of emotional wreckage to sort through.

Have you ever gone through a breakup? No one can get you mad like a significant other can. We yell, we scream, we sometimes even resort to violence. All because the person we "love" didn't behave according to our standards. Our emotions can have us move from mild-mannered individuals to raving lunatics.

One extension of ego is self-identity. Another is self-possession, or should I say possessions of self. In the process of seeking who we are outside of our true selves, what we accumulate in life becomes extensions or aspects of who we are. We are now extending out of self-survival and on to accumulation of possessions. We acquire things that are useful and make life convenient, easing our sufferings. This is just the co-creator nature in us that gives us the desire to do more, want more, and acquire more. We know, deep down, that we can never be satisfied by material gain.

Parents give their children boundaries for this very reason. They know the children would never be satisfied no matter how much is purchased for them. Kids may have a roomful of toys, but if they see a toy that they don't have, they will want that one too. Yes, we do spoil kids to make them happy. We try to give them the things we never had, the things that we feel would have eased our own suffering as children. And guess what happens? They still aren't satisfied! When is enough, enough? What happens is we grow into adults with same exact issues we had as children.

Material possessions are so temporary, suffering will happen quite often if we go that route to try to find our happiness. You know the old saying, you can't take it with you once you're gone, and we agree with that... in theory. But we still try to spend our lives gathering possessions like we can be buried in the casket with all of our stuff. Houses are bought and sold and bought and sold... You worked hard for that house, right? Right. When you die, you intended the house that you purchased to go to your kids to live in and what do they do? Sell it to someone else. It's temporary. That thing that you claimed to be yours was never really yours. You had temporary ownership the whole time. It is, as *The Lion King*, says, the circle of life.

It is the biggest "knowing" that nobody ever talks about. It doesn't really matter how much you do because in a hundred years you will be dead and forgotten. That is what we don't want. Pushed by our burning desire not to be forgotten, we do things to leave our legacy earnestly even though most people aren't even conscious of this fear.

We chase success, fame, make babies, write books, compete in sports, entertain and even break Guinness World Records not to be forgotten. The sad truth is most of us will be forgotten unless you are somebody important like a president unless your name is Jesus Christ, Buddha, or Elijah Muhammad or some other great spiritual leader.

The attachments to our extensions are congruent with our sources of suffering. When our extensions are lost, stolen or damaged the reactions are almost like actual pain to our physical bodies. It makes us physically sick to suffer a loss. Terrible things happen. Our attachment to our things, loved ones, and bodies are the root of our suffering. That is the truth. You want to stop suffering? Disengage from attachment.

There is a theory about why most spiritual leaders are men. Kind of off subject but interesting theory, nonetheless. It is because they don't have the natural attachment that women are wired with. We, the nurturers, the life bearers, have a deep sense of responsibility to care for our offspring and families. The attachments we develop, as women, are chemically induced.

To be free of attachment is to understand the purpose of things, people, and events and to accept it for what it is, nothing more; nothing less. Not saying that is harder for women to do but we, as women, are conditioned for attachment. It comes with our sacrifice and commitment to hold our families together. We acquire that attachment from guiding the souls that we have birthed through life until they can fend for themselves. We condition ourselves to connect and engage in this responsibility, and we pass it on to each generation of women to do the same.

Okay, back to the extensions of ego. If you can accept that this is you, you are ready to move to the next level in life - keep reading. The next stage is all about doing stuff. The ego expands from extensions of me and extensions of mine to the introduction of purpose. The person known as "I," is now moving from becoming a noun to becoming a verb. At this stage of ego maturation, the identity of an individual soul now, is based on what they do in life.

Here, we are focused on the choices, job titles and roles we play in life. We are completely caught up with being a mother or a wife, a husband or a father, a teacher, a lawyer, a musician, or whatever it is that we do for a living. This is not a bad thing at all, this is just us using our power to co-create our universe. We are just wielding the paintbrushes on our personal landscapes. Our egos have to mature in order to progress. You cannot be egoless if you never had ego. However, some people never get beyond this stage.

When this stage has blockages, it is because there was not enough energy accumulated in the previous stage or there were damaging events that blocked the energy of procession. A lot of people never move past the state they are in and it is usually the state that had the biggest effect on them as a child. They are busy feeding the ego's self-esteem with pseudo-accomplishments to pacify whatever voids they feel deep down in the pit of their being.

This stage may not look like an active search for inner peace, joy, and happiness, but it is. Those people who are super achievers and corporate wolves are looking for the same inner peace that the yogis are looking for. Yes, they might be driven by the thirst for power and prestige, but they have had a light bulb moment – they have figured out a certain amount of success will make them content, a certain amount of money will keep them happy, a certain amount of recognition will bring them peace. They are not wrong either. They just have to constantly feed the growing monster they have created. They will never be satisfied...always chasing.

You also have those who are known as rebels. They refuse to be judged by society's standards and they go against what is considered the "status quo". This is also very active search for inner peace and joy. This is everyone's search at the end of the day.

The next stage of the ego is evolving into a higher level of thought. The ego actually starts to take a good look at all the projections and all that it has put out into the universe. The "self," at this point, still isn't ready for absolute truth. Because there was so much done in the previous stages, a sense of arrogance and entitlement sometimes starts to form. Using left brained–thinking, the ego has created two distinct lists: right and wrong. We have seen enough to be convinced and convicted thoroughly of our reality needing to be stable and controlled.

In this stage we become religious. We fight for justice. We speak out against injustices. We march, we meet, we plan, attend rallies... We concentrate on our beliefs and condemn others for their lack of morals. Unfortunately, much suffering comes out of this stage as well because this stability is still only temporary, just like the body and the human experience as a whole. We fight for racial, religious, and gender equality. We fight to save the trees; we fight for more recycling. We fight to maintain our false senses of control we have created. That's a big one. We get overwhelmed by the massive amount of problems. It makes us emotional...sad, angry, and bitter.

We take up causes that are passionate to us. Our eyes are wide open. The world needs healing. There are so many wrongs that need to be corrected. In our eyes, we are doing the world some good; we are making it a better place.

To even write this book is an ego thing. It is my desire to help individuals that are trying to figure out their spiritual journey. My passion is to spread the message that if you have questioned any spiritual information that you have been taught, you are not alone and it is ok. To step outside of what you know and explore new avenues is a scary and lonely feeling. I have been there before, as well.

We are not done with our ego attachments. We must continue to move forward. The ego needs to continue to grow. In order to become egoless, the ego must continue to evolve. The stage that can be observed in the next advancement of ego is called *the stage of knowledge of self*. This is where we start to go inward instead of outward.

Sadly, most of us never make it to this level. In this stage, we begin to reflect on our past and present decisions. We begin to evaluate our lives. This happens only when every other stage has not brought us the contentment and happiness that we have been searching for. There is still a nagging feeling that something is missing from our lives. We begin to take inventory of events, accomplishments, and failures, plans and setbacks, hits and misses.

Although we are still trying to protect the self-image or ego; we begin to question the "why," not just the "what" that happened. Awareness, in its infant stage, is starting to form. Our reactions, although still autonomic, will have more of an in-depth reflection period afterward. We will have hindsight acknowledgment coming from both self-reflection and self-awareness. And you know what they say, hindsight is 20/20.

This stage is the beginning of true searching. One might feel that they have struggled through certain stages and mastered other stages. It's almost like a midlife crisis for the soul. We are still looking for that which is still lost. Even though we haven't realized it yet, the whole time we have been searching for our true selves.

So, who are you? This question might begin to take on a different meaning now, depending on where you are in your ego's development. One thing is clear, the answer is definitely not ego. Who we portray outwardly is not who we really are. It is what we want people to think we are. It is who we wish to be. The tortured soul that struggles and agonizes over life's hardships does not show his or her painstaking face.

The conflict, the evilness, the jealousy and the resentment, the tired and suffering spirit hides, along with numerous skeletons way in the back of your closeted existence. We put on our game face as we face the world. We have to hide the worry, the pain, and frustration. We don't want people to think we are weak, stupid, less than, lazy, ignorant, simple-minded, confused, or thoughtless... the list goes on.

Some of us have worn that face for so long that we really think that what we are doing is what you are supposed to do. It is a habit. That's it; that's all. Something that you've done for so long that it has become second nature. Plus, everyone else is doing it. If you are searching for truth you are trying to go deeper than just this start. You are trying to figure out what this "me" thing is all about, in relation to your place in the Universe.

Why am I here? Why did a Supreme Being make me? What am I supposed to believe? What direction am I supposed to go in?

Asking questions is okay, and being honest about your flaws and failures is even better. Deep down we just want to be loved and accepted. This is the ultimate illusion and the reason you continue to suffer despite what you attempt to change outside. The more you seek outside yourself, the more layers are put on the very thing that has the ability to free you, the soul.

You have moments where you can feel the real "you." These are moments of peace, moments of distraction from daily living, such as taking a walk-in nature, sitting on the beach, praying in church   moments where the inner spirit and God connect and merge. The notion that these moments can only be far and few between if we don't do those specifics things is a falsehood. Spirit and ego can be balanced and the end game is having a life in harmony. This is enlightenment.

-You Are Not Lady Gaga. You Were Not Born This Way-

Being born into a world that is deeply rooted in fear is no one's fault. However, it is everyone's problem. It is not easy to be positive when you're surrounded by negativity. Nowadays, our Western society glorifies violence, overindulgence, sex, and the intake of harmful substances as coping mechanisms. This is all normal for us to see on a daily basis.

Our environment, parental guidance, and predetermined spiritual and physical DNA dictate who we are as children and we carry this over into adulthood. For example, a two-year-old who is just learning the ways of the world is already being exposed to different concepts that he or she will register in his or her mind as good or bad. We are born into a dualistic world and also, we are born with natural instincts from our brain to analyze, compartmentalize and label concepts. A natural trait that we develop is judging situations by gauging the reactions of the people around us. When a two-year-old hears a concept, belief, notion, or theory, they have no choice but to accept it as truth because they haven't lived long enough to have the wisdom of memories for comparison.

If a child is watching Scooby Doo, for example, they will begin to relate to the concept of ghosts as being something scary and are now trained to be fearful of them. They do not yet understand the concept of pretending and animation. So, they have the potential to become fearful of all supernatural phenomena. When they grow up they still have a programmed fear of anything of a supernatural genre.

Does this mean they consciously remember that episode? Probably not. It is stored in their subconscious mind. The memory is not apparent but the effects of the memory can be. I doubt that the creators of this childhood cartoon intentionally meant to program fear but that is what has happened in some cases.

Being exposed to fear programming continues to happen every time we turn on the news. The news mostly reports on negative things and in turn, causes society to focus on negative things. It is a vicious cycle created by something that is seemingly innocent.

Often, our issues we deal with in the present have a lot to do with the past. Any psychologist can attest to that. We all have some type of issue that goes along with our conditioning. So, what is conditioning?

-Conditioned to Believe Conditioning-

We are born perfect. Each one of us is born with no trauma, no immorality, and no negative behaviors. A tiny baby doesn't have the capacity to consider right or wrong. They are innocent and perfect. Imagine this baby's soul as a blank sheet of paper, crisp, fresh and innocent.

Conditioning is all the things we learn along our journey that turns us into "us." Everything we learn becomes etched onto that blank sheet of paper. It is the exposure to behaviors, beliefs, rules, concepts, and perceptions. The first step of conditioning; we are given a name. Then we are taught all our parent's beliefs, habits, and thought concepts as though they are fact. Since this happens immediately we naturally learn not to question things. Our life is our life. We are taught how to eat, walk and talk. We learn right from wrong. We have structured daily schedules. We have boundaries set for us. We are exposed to television, music, family, and religion. We learn gender identification and cultural roles.

We begin to learn society's standards from our parents, teachers, and/or whoever is in charge of our learning. We learn concepts and perceptions that have been passed down from generation to generation. We go to school and learn what the educational system wants us to know and we enter the workforce to provide for ourselves financially. We have social systems in place that give boundaries to the masses such as the judicial system, the political system, entertainment, consumer, religious and educational system.

Things we have absorbed from conditioning contribute to a fear-based way of thinking instead of a love-based way of thinking. We fear the unknown. This instinct is part of our survival. It keeps us cautious, therefore, keeping us alive. Evolution of society has included the evolution of fear which in turn, has made the world the way it is. This is done on purpose as with all things under the laws of duality. The opposite of fear is love and we cannot discover love if nothing pushes us to explore it. There is no learning if we are given the answers.

Conditioning feeds the ego. It receives information and the events, environment, and circumstances we are born into strengthens it. We formulate opinions, perceptions, and develop preferences. Mental suffering stems from not accepting something because it goes against the formulated concept we were conditioned to believe as right or proper.

What we don't understand most of the time gets brushed off. As humans, we understand our own human brain least of all. Ma Yoga Shakti states in "Daughters of the Goddess," "Body, mind, and spirit should be in harmony with each other. The spirit should speak through your intelligence, and intelligence should direct your action."

Unfortunately, for most humans, emotions, ego, and bodily functions dictate our actions first. Why is it easier to be negative than positive? Because we are conditioned to be. It is habit. We are born into a world where the collective consciousness, the mass thought patterns, are based on fear.

We have a "veil of forgetfulness" that is lowered over our souls after we are born. After that, the soul has no knowledge of where it was prior to entering that body. It does not remember its life mission or its purpose for being here. This disconnects us from Source/God from day one, and it seems it is done without purpose. Our duality hides God from God.

The spirit's home is in the subconscious and even though we don't have a conscious memory of everything, the spirit holds all the answers. We, as humans, rarely have access to the subconscious. But there is a purpose why we are here and we do choose this journey. We choose to come here and learn whatever lessons we needed to work on and our whole life is set up to constantly make us aware of those lessons.

Conditioning must be reversed in order to achieve perfect union with Divine Spirit/God. This is the consequences of living in a modern world. There is a misconception that self-image/ego has to be completely destroyed. That is not true. Spirit just must be strengthened in order to be able to keep the ego in check. There are techniques that can aid in this process.

History has shown that denying traditions of society, abstaining from negative behavior and practicing the art of meditation can accelerate the process of enlightenment. In this modern society, however, these are not always possible. We have obligations that cannot be ignored. Dropping everything to meditate constantly is unrealistic. There are other ways to reach Nirvana, the state of divine and constant joy and peace. We actually are already there, but until we realize it, we have to continue to use the mind and the ego to seek outside help and information to help us transition from powerless to spirit-filled.

Methods to aide this process will be explored in due time, but before you can get to where you want to go, you have to know where you came from, who you are. That is why understanding the ego and conditioning is so important. If you are seeking to find yourself, do not bother looking in the mirror because the reflection you see is not the real you.

If the eyes are the window to the soul then the soul is inside of you. You are the one looking at your eyelids when your eyes are closed in meditation. If you close your eyes and let yourself adjust to the darkness you will see that it is not just darkness. There is a whole world inside of ourselves filled with color, lights, fireworks, and visions. The inner you is where you reside. There is a whole world in there. The ego's only job is to help us navigate the outer world, that's it. Somewhere along the way, we let the ego mistakenly think that it was in charge.

-Thinking About What You Are Thinking About-

There are levels of consciousness that are helpful to know regarding ego development. 1. The first is *existence.* Any living being has this level of consciousness. It simply means what it says it is; existing, being alive. Plants, animals, reptiles, mammals and so on function autonomically. This means they don't have purposeful thoughts about decisions; they rely on their instincts. The brain controls body functions and primitive instincts. You don't have to be aware of these activities for them to happen. All life has communication systems even though they may differ from species to species.

The next level is 2. *conscious thought*. This is the level that separates man from all other species of life. Man can consciously think. We are self-aware and aware of our thoughts. We can choose to go with one thought or think another. Even though our thoughts are autonomic most of the time we have a built-in over-ride mechanism located in our frontal lobe that allows us to transcend primitive thought.

The next level is 3. *self-awareness*, the very definition of consciousness. Most of us never make it to this level because even though we consciously choose between the thoughts from our higher and lower natures very few are aware when we are doing it. Most of us are unconscious of our consciousness. To be aware is to simply pay attention to what we do and what we think; to be aware that our thoughts exist.

When you are aware that your thoughts exist and you are the one thinking them you put distance between your ego and your true self. The "witness," the one who watches, now emerges as a separate entity. You have the ability, now, to put space between the event you are witnessing and your reaction to it. This strengthens your ability to be aware.

Going a little deeper, the next level is 4. *self-reflection*. This goes hand in hand with being self-aware, it just takes it a little bit further. So now, not only are you aware that you have conscious thoughts but you analyze the meaning of the thoughts. You can categorize them as autonomic or deliberate. You see how you react and explore the origin of those attitudes. We go deep into the mind at this point, and we begin to transcend our previous egoic state of mind.

Consciousness is like looking into a mirror with another mirror behind you: the reflection is infinite. It as deep as you want to take it, because self-awareness is infinite. You can be aware of your ability to be aware and be self-reflective. This is called self-observant. Observing self while being self-aware will ultimately give you a strong spiritual foundation.

The witness keeps us in a peaceful state of mind because our true state now is so far away from the chaos of everyday life we can participate but still remain still. This is the peace that surpasses all understanding. This is being "in" the world but not "of" the world.

-Know Thyself-

The body is no different than a car. It's the vehicle that propels the soul through this life. Better yet, let's imagine the body as a house. You live in a house, you are not the house. It is a possession. When you sell the house, you do not go back and mow the lawn or take out the garbage. You do not go back and look at the abandoned looking exterior. You simply, move on to the next house.

While you are in this house, you should have some type of knowledge about your own life. The ancient Africans have a saying that was repeated in the movie *The Matrix*: "Know Thyself." This is so important, for if you are to find your own path it has to be based on your own perception. What you relate to, someone else might not even pay attention to. What is meant for you might not be meant for another person. You need to know yourself.

Your true self has been suffering underneath the weight of your false self or ego for a long time. Healing from this can be painful for one who has buried much conflict in his/her subconscious. This is also not an overnight process. Although miracles are ever possible, more often than not it takes multiple years to get rid of all of the dirt that we have shoveled over our souls. This hard work is not optional. This is necessary if you want inner peace.

You have to know what's really under the ego. Don't pretend. What are you really like? Are you impatient? Do you stress out easily? Do you eat when you are upset? You have to know what it is that you do to consciously choose to do something else. You cannot quit something if you hide what you do from everyone, including yourself. You cannot change what you don't acknowledge. We have a very strong power inside of us to help us become better. It is the power to choose.

Our freedom of choice is our most precious gift. As children, it is limited because we are each born into a unique set of circumstances. Once we reach adulthood, those circumstances are still there, unfortunately, and they often dictate the snowball of choices we are faced with making. By this time, we have set labels in place to go along with the choices as either negative or positive. Even though they seem to limit our goals, this is an illusion. Yes, due to childhood circumstances some people have to play the game with the execution of more steps to complete their goal but with determination and focus, you can dominate the game of life regardless of how you started it.

The peace of mind we want to obtain and maintain is no easy feat to accomplish in modern times. There are so many distractions, there are so many examples in our everyday life of unconsciousness; it is easy to forget our true natures and hold on to that blissful joy that comes with awareness.

So, what do you do when all you want is peace and all you see is the opposite? The storms of life can, sometimes, be so relentless that you can barely see your way. It seems like the storms winds and wave can rip the peace right out of your soul like a flimsy umbrella against hurricane conditions. In order to maintain peace, the ego must be trained.

The "I" doesn't ever totally disappear, but it can be trained to know when it is to step to the forefront and when it is to stay in the background. It takes practice, patience, and conscious concentration to achieve this goal. Most of the time, ego will take it upon itself to step forward when nobody even asked for it. This is due to many years of conditioning about personal feelings, possessions, and beliefs. When ego rears its ugly head, it can completely wipe out any evidence of elevated thinking. It will be as though the knowledge acquired on this conscious spiritual journey never even happened.

If stressful emotions do not pass in sufficient time we have options of dealing with it at our disposal. These will be explored in greater detail later on in this book. This is why knowing ourselves is so important. We need to know what works for us, as individuals. Some people are able to pray, listen to spiritual music or use their faith in God to help them feel better but it truly depends on the person.

There are advantages we have that can raise our spiritual vibrations such as music, laughter, nature, socializing, exercise, spiritual practices and meditation among other things. If you know yourself then you will know what you are attracted to. Not only that but what works for one person might not work for another. The ego, in today's modern times, is so strongly developed it just doesn't bow to your every whim overnight. It takes time.

No matter what occurs, remember that everything has a purpose and there is a lesson in every event. Once you are able to keep this truth in your mind's eye, you will know more and more that even in bad situations, there is good present. Once you are able to see the good in all things, you will no longer be a slave to the ego.

-If You Want to Change the Culture, -

Change the Language

We seek to expand our perceptions of reality, to find out why we are here. So why are we here? The answer is, we are here to find out why we are here. Everyone has a purpose. "Without purpose, the people perish." Your purpose made be known or unknown. Your purpose could be your passion. Your passion is what makes you excited when you think about it. If it makes you money, you know, deep down, you would still do it for free. The money, at this point, is an added bonus. Your purpose may be the example you set for others. It may be that you were brought here to guide and protect someone else. Whatever your specific quest is, know thatwe are all here to love one another, love ourselves and to be of service to the Creator.

Your purpose is unique to your soul. Do not try to duplicate someone else's path to peace and happiness. The outward journey, called the spiritual path, will lead you inward where all of the answers lie. The outward journey awakens within you what you already know. Books, such as this one, just give you reminders of what you really already know, because, your soul has taken this journey many, many times previously.

Most spiritual books are written from the writer's perspective of truth and they, usually, give you content without properly defining what they are talking about. Spirituality has so many terms and phrases it can be confusing. You know how humans like to label things. In this section, terms and their meaning will be broken down.

You will find, on the path to spiritual knowledge, there are terms that often inter-related. Meanings can and will vary from person to person. Definitions of certain keywords come from perspectives. The definitions in this book are no different. They just lay the foundation for you to come up with your own personal word descriptions. Accept whatever feels right in your gut. If your intuition disagrees with certain pieces of information, disregard it.

Now, onto the big questions like...why are we here? This answer is just as vast as the various types of spiritual definitions. One theory is that before we were born we, consciously, chose to make the trek down to Earth. We chose our limitations and our life lessons, then, we came here and forgot all of this. So, now, we are saddled with figuring out everything without a cheat sheet. This is our pop quiz, ready or not.

For one soul, organized religion may be the right path for them to reach a higher spiritual enlightenment. For another, they may have evolved past religion. Everything has a purpose. Wiccans have their purpose. Sufism has a purpose; anything and everything can teach a lesson.

Part Two

-Good God Almighty-

If you were to fathom up every rendition of the definition of God and mesh them all together, the result would be quite simple and quite complex at the same time. We would probably end up saying "God" is a supreme spirit that created us and everything around us. An even more simple definition of God would be "I Am" ... Feel free to insert whatever word you want to because God is all of it. God is the energy of existence and non-existence.

God, the father, has, traditionally, been depicted as a white man sitting on a throne high in the heavens. God also has been classified as a spirit which dwells in our hearts. We don't know for sure who is right perhaps both are but that might just be the real beauty of God. God allows you to view God however you choose to.

God the son is known, traditionally, as Jesus, but spiritually, also he represents the individual consciousness that each soul possesses. Jesus had a body and a soul. Jesus is the offspring of God and so are we. Jesus actively participated in the continued evolution of creation and so do we. Whether we are conscious of it or not, we are co-creators.

The Holy Spirit has been taught as being a forceful spirit that is capable of inhabiting our bodies from time to time that can give us healing, power, intuition, and direction. The Holy Spirit can also be the spirit of God, meaning the spirit of supreme consciousness that inhabits all things.

God is such a puny name for "everything" but it is the most common name we have. Our rational mind cannot imagine the "everything" that is everything because most of it is unknown to us. The name is just a name that is understood across different races, religions, cultures, and languages. Say the word, "God," and every person has at least an idea of what you are talking about. Other names we have called God include Creator, Source Energy, Lord, Father, Divine Spirit and Supreme Consciousness. We have heard of Allah, Yahweh, Jehovah and other religious names that represent God the deity. We get confused as to who is right and who is wrong. There is no wrong. We all fashion God to whatever we need God to be.

One person's definition might vary from another person's definition. Even in the absence of a belief system, we are still able to share that love energy with each other. That is all that really matters. Love is the most important thing.

If you were to ask the question, who is God? An omnipresent, omniscience, and omnipotent Deity is a commonly threaded acknowledgement. This is a God who bestows free will, but already knows everything that is going to happen in the future. So, is there really such a thing as free will? It is a paradox. We have free will because we are able to make choices, but the circumstances that dictate the choices are pre-destined. Nothing is by accident.

God is everywhere at once and there is no place God isn't, right? So that means God is where evil is, sickness is, pain is, and suffering is as well, one would logically assume. This topic is so taboo that it is often swiftly condemned as blasphemy. The average person usually believes that suffering does not come from God, but this is a complete contradiction of the belief that everything comes from God and to the belief that God is all-powerful. God is all-powerful but not powerful enough to prevent tragedy or failure? This leads us to one of the oldest and perhaps, greatest of all the paradoxes. Why does God allow suffering?

It won't be easy tackling this answer. One possible reason we can assume that God "the deity" would allow suffering is because suffering gives us the push that we need to grow spiritually. It has a greater good even though it doesn't feel good, and it isn't perceived as good. In the traditional story of good and evil, you have a God and you have a Devil. One represents good and one represents evil. Then you have the argument that God doesn't create evil, the Devil does. But who created the Devil? Well, if you argue, God didn't know that Lucifer would turn to evil when he created him, it has to be asked, well, is God omniscient or isn't he?

So, God is responsible for evil by default and in the story, the Devil does serve a purpose. We, as humans, just fear what we don't understand. It may take a while to let this sink in because we are conditioned to believe that God is perfect. Knowing this doesn't make God imperfect, it makes God's purpose for us even more prominent. We are born into a world of duality. We cannot know what good is if we have never experienced evil. We cannot know joy if we have never experienced pain and we cannot know enlightenment if we have never experienced suffering.

Another big question is, "Why are we here?" Well, most religious or spiritual origins have God existing as only consciousness, not matter, before anything existed. This consciousness only ever knew the awareness of being this consciousness. The thought of coexistence and experienced entered the mind of this consciousness and matter was created.

This allowed the consciousness we call God or the Creator to experience itself. It evolved and continues to evolve moment by moment. Two popular stories of creation are the creation story in the Bible and the Big Bang theory. The creation story is a detailed account of how the earth was created and the Big Bang theory is a scientific version of the creation of the universe. There is a saying that goes, "Nothing is for certain." Whether these theories are fact or fiction is irrelevant because we don't really know for sure. Just because we have passed information down for eons doesn't mean it is accurate.

Quantum physics has disproved the basic laws of physics because when scientists studied sub-atomic particles, those sub-atomic particles defied the laws of physics already in place. The point is, theories have the flexibility to allow for change. Beliefs are much harder to change because our minds have a habit of rejecting what they don't understand.

Usually "God" or whatever you call that supreme spirit is worshipped or acknowledged in three ways. 1. The first way is having multiple deities that represent multiple righteous principles and 2. there is the "God within" and 3. the "God without". This is the second and third way God is view respectively. The "God without" is a separate supreme entity from ourselves that has its own personality and makes its own decisions. It governs us in all ways and decides our fate in the afterlife.

The "God within" has no separation between God, ourselves or anything else. All is from God; therefore, all is God, including ourselves. We can achieve enlightenment and find peace in any of these paths.

Viewing God as separate entity leads us to believe that we are powerless and we have to constantly search and seek outside of ourselves when the answers have been hidden within us. We have had access to the cheat sheet for the test the entire time! We simply never knew.

The above explanation of God in detail is that God originated as a consciousness that expanded. Evolution and creation are a result of this consciousness wanting to experience itself. Fast forward to the human soul consciousness; this is still "God consciousness" wanting to experience itself. To fully experience itself, it separated and hid itself from itself. Why? Who knows for sure? Maybe God likes a good game of hide and seek.

Which means, in turn, that our lives are nothing but a game. Some might take offense to this notion. The perils of life are no joke to the one that is engaged in the struggle. How can life be a game? Life is God's ultimate game of hide and seek with itself. God created man in

God's image, the image of the divine consciousness, then he/she/it hid this truth in our subconscious and we only get to feel a glimpse of what is really on the other side of the veil of forgetfulness.

We are given self-awareness and animalistic instincts in the same brain. We are given free will and dropped off here to experience existence. Why? So, God incarnate, (us), could explore and possibly discover God all over again. It's not like we aren't aware of this before we get here. This third dimension of duality makes us feel really separate from God but we are not. We happily accepted this challenge to become lost in the wilderness and rediscover home. Why not? Finding God is a great joy and realizing you are it is an even greater joy. Reuniting with the stream of unconditional and infinite love, which is God, is the greatest joy.

To know God is to know self and to know self is to know God. To know God is to know the true identity of self that is likened to a perfect diamond covered with a coat of mud and hard dirt. If someone were to hand a random stranger a lump of coal and say, "Take care of this, it's valuable." The stranger's first reaction would probably be to drop it or throw it away. If the giver fails to inform the stranger that there is a priceless, perfect diamond lying at the center of all that gunk, the stranger would just assume that it is worthless.

Our souls/spirits play the role of the diamond in this example and the outward projection of ego/personality is the muddy covering. We, as humans, are just like the stranger who receives the lump of coal. We have limited information at first glance and we see the outside and think that is all there is. We accept what we see because knowledge of self has been hidden.

So, we carry this lump daily. Some people never see anything more than a lump of coal. That is the drawback of this life. It is very likely that you may come here with every intention of finding the Creator and leave here never accomplishing that task. They, who are ignorant, dismiss the nugget as something that isn't worth caring for. They neglect it, muck and murk it up further, are ashamed of it because of its outward appearance, some people will even deny owning it. But, every now and then, there is a glint of light visible from underneath the thick coating.

It isn't even noticeable to everyone. Some people peep that shine and this sparks their interest to further investigate. You have those nosy individuals who intuitively know that appearances aren't always what they seem. You have others who, logically, have sense enough to know there is a reason they were given this hard nugget.

Curious souls will begin to see if the dirt and grime can be cleaned off. They will engage in this tedious task, using all sorts of tactics because even with just a glimpse of the light, they know there is value in the obstructed object. It may be long and grueling. There are some who will grow tired and give up on their quest. Then, there are others who have partially removed the coating and see the beauty underneath shining through.

They are satisfied with the progress they have made and will spend the rest of their days admiring a half-clean diamond. "Spirit", previously hidden, can shine with a prism of brilliant colors on display and stand in its full glory as it has always been, perfect and priceless. All you have do is clean it off.

-Mind, Soul, and Spirit – The True Trinity-

This part of the book is about redefining old phrases in a new light.

The definition of the word, Trinity, has a biblical origin. It is the cornerstone of the Christian belief system. It is believed that God has three aspects: the father, the son and the Holy Spirit. That could very well be true, but there is another trinity that we should not disregard. This true trinity is you...you ARE the complete package: a perfect reflection of God's creation.

God the Father is equal to the "Mind" aspect of your being. It is always present and in charge most of the time. The son represents the body. This is the part that makes you human. Jesus incarnated to earth to fulfill a purpose and in order to do that he needed a body. We do the exact same thing. The Holy Spirit is spirit personified and in keeping up with the traditional Holy Ghost, our inner spirit only appears every once in a while, but it is extremely powerful.

There is a wide assortment of people out there who belong to a religion and don't know the definition of the word, Religion. Spirituality and religion have always been terms that are interchangeable but there are slight differences between the two. Religion is based on rules and traditions while spirituality is based on choice, free will and what feels right according to one's own personal connection with Source.

Spirituality represents applying structure or non-structured principles to one's life that lead to a closer union with God and a deeper understanding of existence. It focuses on the individualized relationship between man and Source. Spirit connects to Source through intuition. It is the process of seeking God from within.

Religion is a structured relationship between man and Source. It is a process of looking outward and honoring the God represented outside of ourselves. Rules, traditions, and rituals, created by Man, unite us in our seeking, serving, and appreciation of God. Religion is majority based; spirituality is minority based. Both religion and spirituality can be monotheistic or polytheistic.

-You Gotta Have Faitha, Faitha, Faith…

Just Like George Michaels-

When following the conscious path of spirituality, we shift from a state of autonomic reaction to precise awareness. There is a passage in the Bible that talks about the "peace" that surpasses all understanding. This means peace that is unwavering and unfaltering. There are few in this world that have actually reached this level and even fewer that can maintain it on a constant basis. Most don't even realize such a thing is possible.

There are some elders that have achieved Nirvana but not without dedicating many years to the goal. The truth is nirvana, "heaven on earth", is inside of each one of us and can be reached by anyone, anytime.

This is what the spiritual path is all about. We are going through this whole song and dance on the outside to eventually steer our path

Real Life Enlightenment   Part Two

inward so we can reach this ever-peaceful state in a chaotic world. It is definitely a road less traveled but the benefits not only outweigh the risks...there are no risks. Imagine remaining completely stress-free, no matter what situation arises.

We now know that conditioning and the ego have eluded truth and have made life very hard. We end up seeking this path motivated by suffering, frustration, desperation, and a deep desire for truth. The real deal is that there are no cut-and-dry, clear set rules for achieving enlightenment. What works for one soul may not work for another. That is why we have free will.

The spiritual path is all about finding out what works for you; however, there are some universal truths that can help everyone. The journey to consciousness is not an overnight trip. It requires desire, will, and determination. As long as desire and openness to receive are present, the universe will put the right information in your hands.

Since we are all groomed from birth to think a certain way, the truth seeker must go inside, shift through all the mess and bravely discard what is not needed. You have to be open to the endless possibilities of spiritual knowledge and wisdom. You must hold on to the faith in God, the "I Am", the Creator, the universe, etc.... to give you what you need. And you need faith in yourself! You are smart enough to figure this out.

Hell, this isn't even your first time here! If you close yourself off mentally and spiritually, the information you desire and require will hit a brick wall of resistance and never get a chance to take root and grow. Spirituality doesn't even have to be taken that seriously. It's about "following your bliss". Indulging in this path has so many great benefits. Who doesn't want to be at peace all the time?

Want to know a secret? The universal battle between good and evil is happening inside of our heads. Yup...it is. Let that one sink in for a minute. It originates in our perception. Good, bad, right, and wrong, are an illusion because they are learning tools. They are part of the dualistic nature of this third-dimensional existence. Catalysts are waiting to motivate every decision.

We have perceived these catalysts as good or evil based off of cause and effect and how that makes us feel; however, these catalysts are necessary for us to make choices. Choices birth learning experiences and every choice is an opportunity for growth. Since perception is unique to each individual, understanding self is essential to growth.

Why do you think the way you do? What happened to you that made you formulate opinions on different matters? Exploring your inner workings will give you a foundation in truth and aid you in developing a willingness to accept the truth, which in turn will make your outlook more serene.

Unwillingness to accept the truth is at the root of suffering. The truth is "life" is going to happen. Things are going to happen. The mind knows and tells us what should and shouldn't be occurring based on our conditioning, which in turn, develops our perception. The inability to surrender to what is going on at any given moment often leaves us feeling bitter and negative. We develop a "me against the world" or "The whole worlds against me" attitude.

Acceptance is the key to freedom. That is the secret no one has ever told you...because most people don't know this. Acceptance is seeing what's in front of you and acknowledging that whatever it is - is. It is knowing in your heart that what you are experiencing is divine in nature and meaningful even if it doesn't feel good. We are not taught this. We are taught most times, that if it feels good, it is wrong.

We are taught to swim against the current instead of just go with the flow. But swimming against the current is rooted in the fear that if we go with the current, it will take us somewhere we don't want to end up. We are fighting against the possibility of suffering but in truth, suffering is a mindset, not a reality. Fear of suffering causes suffering.

Ok, let's read that one again. Fear of suffering CAUSES suffering. Nothing else. And fear is a slap in the face of faith. Faith is the forerunner of the spiritual journey. It rides out on its white horse on the front line of battle.   It doesn't cower in the back hoping that nobody hits it.   Faith is fearless.

It takes faith to believe in God since there is no concrete evidence of a "God" or a "Creator." Every theory about God has come from the soul of humans. It's a theory that we cultivated into a belief. We are introduced to the notion of a "God" mostly as children and most of us stick to it because of the feeling we get. It just feels right in our guts. Now, some of us, "deep and nosy" thinkers have begun to look at the specifics and get an eerie, unshakable feeling that something isn't all the way right with our beliefs.

Some of us haven't got the logistics worked all the way but we just HAD to be know-it-alls and seek truths for ourselves. We set out on personal pilgrimages to find the "Holy Grail" of God-knowledge. Stepping out on faith with no structure is a lot like entering a forest with no map. As soon as you step out of your comfort zone, you immediately feel lost. That out of control, "I don't what is what anymore" feeling is extremely overwhelming. What do most people do next? They freak out. The uncomfortable feeling of uncertainty leads to unhappiness which leads to emotional pain and suffering. This might not seem like it is part of a spiritual plan but it is. It is called finding the joy through pain. Oh, the irony...

Seeking happiness outside of yourself is actually harder than seeking it inside yourself. Outside happiness is so temporary that you have to constantly search for and maintain it. However, the diligent one that remains focused on the task can complete it. This can lead to Enlightenment as well. There are many roads to Enlightenment. Enlightenment can be defined as an inner peace; a blessed state of mind that has the absence of suffering. Knowing and feeling its presence brings endless joy. It doesn't cut out negative events but it allows us to have a choice whether to feed into negative emotions or not. This is literally heaven on earth. A person who has the ability to not suffer during uncomfortable occurrences has a rare gift. It is rare because so many people have already written this natural ability off as impossible. But, it is possible if you understand how the mind, spirit, and soul function.

-The Spiritual Table-

The untrained mind is governed mostly by the ego, but it can be trained to be ruled by the soul/spirit. Although the mind is made up of conscious thought, a huge portion of the mind is subconscious, unaware and unconscious thinking. The subconscious belongs to the spirit/ soul. The spirit and the soul are interchangeable in areas and these similarities plug both into the subconscious mind. This is what is activated when we get hypnotized. We are not consciously aware of this portion of our mind but it contains the Akashic records.

The Akashic records are literally the storage of the mind of God. It contains all of the information that has ever existed and will ever exist. If God is the macrocosm, the soul is the microcosm. The conscious mind deals with emotions, some memories, opinions, and thoughts. The subconscious mind is the keeper of dreams, the pain body, DNA memory, past life memories and buried memories. The conscious body navigates this world; the subconscious body keeps the biological systems together and functioning. The soul houses all of this.

Akasha is the spirit, the animator, and the awareness. It is universal because all of our spirits come from the same place, God's spirit. It is the ether, the direct connection to the Almighty Creator. Its energy animates the body along with the soul. The spirit is the part of God that makes YOU God. Spirit is also defined as the universal substance that everything is made of. The spirit holds the blueprint for the soul. It is in charge of the functions of the right brain. It is timeless, ageless and infinite. It is the God that existed before existence existed and it is inside of you.

There are different realms or dimensions of spirit. For example, humans reside in the third dimension, but angels and departed souls dwell in other realms or vibrations. Everything is made of spirit, including everything you can see and everything you can't see. The human eye can only see some of what is in the visual field, so there is plenty out there that we cannot see.

For example, we cannot see gamma rays, radio waves, and ultraviolet waves but they are around us all the time. There is also a hierarchy of the spirit because there are different densities of vibrations of spirit. The denser the spiritual matter the more solid it manifests. The lighter the spirit the more invisible it is to the naked human eye.

The spirit is the thing that connects all things to each other. Energetically it bonds living things together, but, it is also the building blocks of the existence of all matter. Even though we can't physically see it, there is spirit in a table. The difference between living and nonliving material is the rate that the molecules spin. The table actually is moving! We just can't see it with our eyes.

The atoms in all matter vibrate while they spin. To break it down even further is to actually look at what an atom consists of. Atoms are made of electrons orbiting around a central nucleus, made up of protons and neutrons. There is space in between the nucleus and the spinning electrons. There is also space between atoms. As a matter of fact, science has proven that an atom has 99% dead space inside of it. Electrons move at such a high speed that they portray the illusion of solidity. This fact scientifically proves that reality is an illusion.

Ok, back to the table...so, all these spinning particles are packed in so tightly together that what we feel, feels solid. That table is made of the same stuff we are made from. Molecules, atoms, and subatomic particles all came from the same place; from creation; from the mind of God.

The soul is the seer, the silent watcher, and the silent partner. It is the witness to the awareness. Our soul keeps the imprint of memories of our previous states of existence and is the individual piece of spirit that is customized to fit a particular experience or body. It is a part of God like everything else but it does not remember this so it feels separate from God. It creates the dualistic nature of humans.

The soul gives a person a sense of individualism. It is where the imprint of our personal experiences lives. Although large-seeming to us, it is but a drop in the vast ocean of God's consciousness.

The soul is infinite just like the spirit, but it is not shaped or made like the spirit. It has multiple experiences simultaneously and spreads across infinite realms and parallel universes. In each realm, a piece of the soul is left behind as the souls moves onward, therefore, it has infinite clones. These clones aren't separate pieces. They are pieces of a whole. This is just another example of the evolution of the Divine Consciousness/God.

For example, when a soul leaves earth it enters the etheric realms with its etheric body. Souls of loved ones greet our souls. They left this piece of their soul behind for our benefit just like we will leave a piece of our soul in the spirit realm for someone else's benefit. Another part of their soul has moved on to the next journey, whether it be higher learning, teaching, guiding a soul, being stuck between realms or reincarnating back to earth or even traveling some other place in the multi-verses.

Time is a manmade construct. We have developed the concept of time from the rotation of the earth and the rotation around the sun. In spirit, there is no such thing as time. All of our soul's incarnations and unfolding's are really happening simultaneously. This is how heaven, hell, ghosts and reincarnation can co-exist. Please remember, these definitions of soul and spirit can vary from person to person based off of personal perception. These definitions are not absolute truths.

Here Today, Gone Tomorrow-

The soul houses the unique qualities and traits that each one of us is given in our life experience. It helps shape our personalities for this specific life journey and previous life journeys. It gives animation to the body and when it leaves the body we are no longer thought to be alive. We are dead to outside observation. Death is thought to be the end of life and that's it. We are born, that's the beginning, and we die, that's the end.

The debate about what happens after we die has probably been active since the very beginning of human existence. Since we have no official truth about what happens next, we have to treat the concept of a possible afterlife the same way we treat proof of the existence of God. Our conclusions are based off pure speculation, faith and what resonates within our hearts.

We use religious texts, philosophical theories, and even near-death experience survivor stories to come up with afterlife theories. We, also, look back in history to ancient civilizations and read their speculations about the afterlife. Honestly, spiritual truths can and should be personal, and it can be any mesh of knowledge that best suits you. We can use our past teachings, gut feelings and/or faith to figure out what concept is best. We try to come to a conclusion about what happens because the act of death is one of the scariest things we, as a species, have ever had to deal with. It even looks painful!

Death's spiritual definition is a transition of the soul and spirit from one level of vibration to the next. People have found various ways to cope with death, often, based on cultural traditions. Grief shows different faces and we, as humans, have serious issues when it comes to a permanent exit from this life. For one, it's completely unpredictable!

We hear all the time about death from the news, the tv, the radio, and word of mouth. We all know at least one person who has died unexpectedly. That shit is scary. You could be walking down the street, minding your own business, and seriously, just drop dead. Gone! Who is looking forward to disappearing and becoming a memory? Nobody.

The fact that we are born with sand running from our life's "hourglass" sucks big time. Watching the news only makes it worse. You hear about car accidents, babies dying, fires, bombs being dropped on people among other horrible things. We are fed these images at a young age, and we are taught to fear death and dying. By adulthood, multiple funerals and generalized fears have driven our fears to such a deep level that it is now unconscious. That means that the fear is now automatic and it is happening whether you are aware of it or not. To make matters worse, certain religions have very bleak views regarding death, dying and the afterlife.

Strict judgments and swift punishments are waiting for those who mess up while down here on earth according to some religious leaders. We attend funerals and memorials, hoping that soul is in a better place, grieve for our loss and at the same time, face our own mortality every single time. As much as we, believers in a God, would like to pretend we have knowledge of an absolute truth, the truth is we have no idea why things happen the way they happen and why they even happened in the first place. This cycle reinforces our fear of the unknown. Nobody can absolutely say what happens after we die because once we are gone for an extended amount of time, there is no returning to report back whether we are right or wrong regarding theories.

On top of that, there are a bunch of different explanations to what happens after we die and sometimes they don't match each other. For example, to dig deeper into the above definition of the soul, this question is presented: how can there be such a thing as a ghost that haunts a building if that soul is being reincarnated? How can your mother be in heaven if the psychic medium tells you that she is standing behind you during the session? We have a limited understanding of the spirit/soul and its functions, especially after it is no longer in a body. If we look to intellectual consciousness for answers we still come up empty-handed. Or will we?

In P.M.H Atwater's book, Beyond the Light, she introduces a man named Mellen-Thomas Benedict to the near-death community and chronicles his ninety-minute trip to the other side. Benedict's account of his near-death experience recounts the details of his "conscious" death, meaning he was aware of himself and his pre-death personality was still intact. He asked his appointed guides to answer certain questions. These answers also came to a fifteen-year-old girl, my daughter, through divine revelation. (Shameless plug).

Thomas Benedict was shown that the soul has capabilities of being in more than one place at the same time. We would see it as pieces of the soul but the word "pieces" indicate separateness and the soul is never really separate from itself or God.

If we were to use a story as an allegory of the death experience, the Harry Potter series is useful. In the final book of the Harry Potter series, *Harry Potter, and the Deathly Hallows*, Dumbledore charges Harry and his friends with finding Horcruxes, which are pieces of Voldemort's soul that he broke off into pieces and hid in remote and undetectable places. This is in a children's fiction book but Thomas Benedict and others have confirmed that this isn't too far from the truth regarding the evolution of the soul cycle and the anatomy of the soul. The soul is a pure descendant of the essence of the Divine Consciousness. As it steps down through the layers of creation, it finds direction. The soul regresses to act as the creator experiencing itself and then, evolves back to the absolute oneness that is God. Along the way, the energy never dies, it just changes form.

If you were to take the example of one soul's journey, there can be no specific conclusion to what will happen after they die. Beliefs here on earth play a part in shaping that soul's afterlife. We have heard assorted stories from near death survivors and their stories are pretty similar. The soul leaves the body, goes through the tunnel of light, meets loved ones, experiences a life review and then, gets its next assignment. The bonds of love created from this recently expired lifetime cause part of the soul to stay behind in the spirit world to be close to and ready to receive future loved ones when they cross over.

Another part of the soul reincarnates and still, another part of the soul that is further down the evolutionary road acts as an overseer and guide to the newly incarnated soul. The soul is able to split apart as many times as needed yet still remain intact. Imagine how many lifetimes a soul has gone through! No matter how many times our loved ones have been here, they will still be able to greet us when we cross over. Have you ever met a person who swears they know you? They probably do. Their soul recognizes your soul.

This is just a theory that ties reincarnation to heaven and to the spirit world. Since dimensional levels of existence are infinite, a soul can do this forever. Gaining an understanding of the soul and the spirit gives us a deeper understanding of the Creator. The soul cannot be fully free while engulfed in fear. We know what we wanted deep down when we chose a non-traditional spiritual path; we seek peace of mind. We want to be good people. We want to understand God better.

-Remain Calm, It's Just a Misunderstanding-

Enlightenment is the goal at the end of the conscious spiritual path. It is the awakening of one's inner self to one's own truth by decreasing the ego and expanding the perception of reality through the third eye. Once here, the truth is discovered to be love, love is God, God is love and both are infinitely available at all times. To say Enlightenment is the end is still not entirely accurate because this is still a process that can grow more and more while we are engaged in it. This process also releases old fears and helps us understand the bigger picture that we usually don't see when it comes to the world and humankind's existence in it. As we grow spiritually, we learn to see through the illusions of the mind.

Our thoughts, emotions, feelings, and experiences that make up our identity are only temporary fixtures in the grand design. We also can nurture our own personal relationships with our own personal God. This spectrum begins at only being able to recognize God as an outside source, separate from ourselves and ends with being able to see God in all things and believing everything is interconnected and is an aspect/extension of God, including ourselves.

The conscious spiritual path is a personal, customized path to Enlightenment. Everyone is on this path whether they recognize it or not. No two souls are on exactly the same path but all our paths share commonalities. The "seeking" path leads towards the evolution of the mind, body and spirit unit based on information provided directly by universal "God" influences. It is the truth seekers' road to awareness, freedom, joy, and bliss, and it feels fantastic.

There are misconceptions out here, even taught in religious doctrines that say it is wrong to go against what has been taught in the past. Why is this a fact? What makes this a fact and who said this was a fact anyway? We have been conditioned to fear God and the wrath of God if we break a rule. In order to get to enlightenment, we have to conquer the doubt of misconceptions. Organized religion has offered truths that might not apply to everyone.

One of the absolute biggest misconceptions about a spiritual path is that seeking truth is wrong in God's eyes. We can ask questions in school, we can ask questions amongst each other but we can't ask God a simple question? Kids ask questions all of the time and sometimes the answers will be "That is none of your business." As adults, we know that sometimes children are not mentally ready to understand the answer. But, some of us, who are spiritually advanced enough to understand the answers ARE ready to receive them.

Why do we think that God's business is so personal and mysterious that we can't even say, "Um, excuse me, God, I know you are busy and all but I have a question..."? What type of unconditionally loving God has no patience for a question? This is a rule that some will not question. It will not matter to them. Their logic will be, "God said it, who are we to question it?" and that is fine for them. But, there are some of us who will not let sleeping dogs lie. The first step to spiritual freedom is, "Question Everything."

The second biggest misconception is that there is only one path to God. This is reinforced constantly in organized religions and taught in the strictest of dogmatic practices. We are taught rules...hard rules...rules that are so hard that they are broken by the very people who teach them. So why are the odds stacked so highly against us? We are down here trying to follow these rules that sometimes, go against our very nature. We are doomed to fail. We were created flawed and then we are told we are held accountable for something that was passed down to us? Why would a self-less and unconditionally loving God be so cruel?

Here is a thought: say an Eskimo life in some remote part of the world and never has the opportunity to learn about Jesus and his teachings. When that Eskimo dies he has to go to Hell because he never got "saved"? How is that fair? How is that his fault?

These are the questions we MUST ask.

A misconception is that you can't love God if you don't fear God. Do you have to fear your father to obey him? Maybe...it depends on the kid. Some kids are naturally rebellious and need a good dose of fear to make them straighten up and fly right. Others are mild-mannered and only need a firm "talking to", and still, there are others who will do anything to please their "Father" because they want their "Father" to be proud of them.

All spiritual rules don't apply to all people the same way.

There is a misinformation that all spiritual rules apply to all people the same way and for the same purpose. We come here on different levels just like in school. Someone in kindergarten is not going to understand lessons for someone in fifth grade. We are going to decipher spiritual information according to all own perceptions and all our perceptions are different. So which path is the right one? That is a major question we have to ask ourselves. The answer is whatever path we are attracted to. Nothing is going to happen that isn't supposed to happen. Have faith in your path. It will unfold for you...and it will feel right.

Imagine the spiritual path is like an actual dirt road path leading into a forest preserve. As you venture into the woods, the deeper you move along the scenery, the denser the streets become, obstructing the light from the sun. You are walking a dirt path that is connecting and intertwining with other dirt paths. You have no map but you know you have to keep moving forward.

The search for truth is the motion of forwardness along the path. The mind is now wandering through a vast array of knowledge with no definite signs or arrows pointing to freedom. Each of the trees represents a piece of truth that was once hidden but now is presenting itself as information. There are many entrances down into the thick of the forest and likewise, there are many exits on the other side of the clearing. Each path is specific to the person perceiving it.

Sometimes, there are dead ends, sometimes, there are forks in the road. Some paths merge at places and split apart at other places. Some paths intertwine and intersect. Some paths are more difficult than others. They might lead to a steep slope, an obstruction or even poisonous plant life. This is extremely difficult to navigate because of the overwhelming feeling of being lost. This is why people decide that they need a teacher, guru, or guide. They look to someone who has been down this path before can provide a sense of direction. While this might be true, no one can decipher every single tree for you. It is your personal forest. The information that presents itself and the events that unfold are perfectly aligned with your soul's journey.

A true guru or teacher will tell you to trust the universe for answers. Your truth matches your own perception. It is customized, made to fit and tailored to your own unique experience. So, as you explore, do so with open eyes. Pay attention to the information that is presented and how it is presented. Do not focus on who is giving it. That is not important.

The universe will customize its language to speak to you in the language you understand and are ready to receive. Pay attention to the signs. They can come as dreams, books, conversations, coincidences, even television, music, and movies. The Almighty can and will use anything as a vessel. You might come across phrases that you, perhaps, will not understand the moment you hear it, but later, after reflection, it will begin to make sense. If it doesn't resonate with your spirit, don't worry about it. Perhaps, it will later or perhaps, it was not meant for you.

The key to navigation is trust and faith. If you have asked God to reveal the truth to you, you have to trust God to deliver the goods. It doesn't matter that you are doubting specific definitions of spiritual terms or have realized that belief systems are flawed. We come from a place of strength and our daily survival in this harsh world just proves our strength that much further.

We can potentially wander aimlessly for a few days or even years, depending on where we are in our spiritual growth. The pace can accelerate or slow down. It is difficult not to get frustrated and begin to judge the rate at which we receive information or compare our journey to someone else's. We may feel like it is going too fast or too slow. We come from a "hurry up and wait" society. Be patient, dear ones.

Eventually, if we stay at it, the forest will reveal a path that will become clearer and cleaner under our feet. In the forest of truth, all paths are connected and pre-destined. You will gradually learn how to be comfortable with your own path. It is all trial and error until you learn how to quiet your mind and hear the Divine whisper the directions.

So why even go down into the forest in the first place? It sounds hard to someone who isn't familiar with hiking. Do I have the correct gear? Which trail is the right one to choose? Which one is the best path? Which one is the easiest path? All human souls are on this path, whether they are aware of it or not. We are all on the path. We didn't choose this path, it chose us. If we keep seeking spiritual truth with faith and an open mind we will eventually find what we seek. Seek and ye shall find, says a holy book. If you go looking for God, he/she/they/it is bound to show up.

So why even go down into the forest in the first place? All roads lead to God eventually. The only thing that happens to the forest the further you go is it gets bigger because consciousness is infinite. As the puzzle pieces fall into place, the puzzle gets bigger. The rabbit hole can go as deep as you want it to go. God is infinite, the forest is infinite; the rabbit hole is infinite...that is the way it is set up.

You have the free will in this lifetime to stop at any moment and settle for what feels right in that moment of your journey. If Buddhism speaks to your spirit, it is ok to say, I have found what I am meant to be. I am a Buddhist. There are a few of us seekers who like the game of seeing how far the rabbit hole goes just for the sheer enjoyment of the game. And there is nothing wrong with that either.

The conscious spiritual journey is about the relinquishing or the unlearning of fear and the acceptance of true love back into our hearts. After all of these years existing in this modern society the act of unlearning fear is not going to happen overnight. Fear has been peddled as propaganda for the longest time. Wanting a spiritual awakening and instantaneous enlightenment is great but most times, it is a process. It takes as long as it takes but know this, there is no such thing as an end to gaining spiritual knowledge. There will never be a statement made saying, "I have learned all that there is to learn. I'm done."

Spiritual knowledge is just as infinite as the Creator itself. There is no end. Just stay open and have faith that you will receive what you are meant to receive. We want to be like Buddha, or like Gandhi, or like Jesus but we can't have the reward without the work. We have to have the will, the courage and then add faith, patience, and love to that. We have to have patience when it comes to our own shortcomings and refrain from judging others and ourselves. If we judge ourselves, it leads to negative thoughts, frustration, loss of faith and eventually back to where we started.

To know thyself is to know the Creator. You can find the Almighty through seeking self-understanding and self-love. If you want to honor God, honor yourself. If you want to love God, love yourself. There is no such thing as a wrong turn on your path. Everything happens in Divine Order. No matter what is in front of you, it is part of your path. Trust it, follow it and be grateful for it.

-What You Seek Is Seeking You – Rumi-

If God is the macrocosm, the soul is the microcosm. This gives extra meaning to the phrase, "As above, so below," a term in Hermeticism. We are the little forms of God. We have reviewed definitions for functions of the different aspects of spirit. The conscious spirit feels a connection with source, the unconscious spirit houses the Akashic records. The Akashic records are a non-physical library that contains all recorded events from past, present, and future. The conscious mind deals with emotions, opinions, known memories and thoughts, the unconscious mind is the keeper of dreams and unknown memories. The conscious body navigates this world, the unconscious body keeps the biological systems together and functioning. The soul houses all of the systems. Once we can identify who does what internally we are now ready to turn our spiritual journey inward.

This is what the spiritual path is all about. We are going through this whole song and dance on the outside to eventually steer our path inward so we can reach this ever-peaceful state in a chaotic world. It is definitely a road less traveled but the benefits not only outweigh the risks...there are no risks. Imagine remaining completely stress free, no matter what situation arises. There are some universal truths that can help everyone no matter what teachings or principles you have chosen to follow. The journey to consciousness is not an overnight result. As long as desire and openness to receive are present, the universe will put the right information in your hands.

Since we are all groomed from birth to think a certain way, the truth seeker must go inside, sift through all the mess, and bravely discard what is not needed. Without these steps we remain in a box, stay asleep to the truth, and end up being controlled. Knowledge is power and it takes bravery and courage to step into a "truth seeker's" path.

On the other side of the same coin to be a "truth seeker" is a path that is not meant for everybody. There are those that will try to abandon their core teachings only to find out it is what is meant for them to hold on to. You will find out which road is the right one if you trust in God, the "I am," the Creator, the universe, etc.... to give you what you need. If you close yourself off mentally and spiritually, the information you desire and require will hit a brick wall of resistance and never get a chance to take root and grow. Spirituality doesn't even have to be taken that seriously. It's about doing what feels right and following your bliss.

There are different rules for different people. Hopefully, in seeking truth our lessons will teach us to have more love, more compassion and less judgement. When we love each other, we love the Creator because we are all drops from the ocean of the Creator's mind. Looking and searching for truth is not an insult to Divine Source. It is us expressing our birthright; the ability to be powerful Co-creators.

Since we are drops of water running into the spiritual river that runs into the spiritual ocean, no matter how strong the current, the Holy Spirit/our intuition is a life vest that will keep us afloat and pull us along the way to the journey back home. Since we always forget our course once we get to earth anyway, if a soul strays completely off their charted course, it is ok. The more we reincarnate, the more we grow in spirit.

Earth is like a pop quiz and after death, we get to sit with the teachers and go over the answers together. Yes, there is judgement to point out the mistakes but we get to participate in the process as co-creators and we also get to charter our course for the next life or the next assignment according to multiple spiritual teachings. Your afterlife is based on whatever beliefs you pick up here. If you hold onto that fateful position that you fed into while you were alive, you are more likely to experience it in death, per NDE survivors. So, yes, if you believe you are subject to a hell, you will end up experiencing one. You are creating it for yourself.

We need to come here so that we can grow spiritually. There are other assignments our souls would like to indulge in but we need to master certain positive attributes. So, we come here and go through however many life cycles as needed to achieve our goal. Earth is the perfect place to do that because of its dualistic nature and its cycles of karma. According to the Reluctant Messenger website, there is a legend that says this was not always so.

There once was a story of paradise, many eons ago, human souls were free to ponder their spiritual growth free from suffering. They did not have free will because their world did not have the dualistic reality. There was no "hot to a cold", no "wrong to a right." They did not have the veil of forgetfulness that erased the previous eons of memories. They knew from whence they came and they knew where they were going. They remembered their previous lifetimes. They knew their relationship as it pertains to the Almighty Creator. They knew their lessons, their consequences, and their purposes.

Guess what happened in that story? Humans got lazy. They didn't move along the evolutionary path that was created for them because they were too comfortable. Imagine comparing this story to a kid in school whose father is the principal. The father loves him unconditionally and never punishes him. This child knows that no matter what he does, his dad will not discipline him because of his actions. After a while, the kid will feel like he can do what he wants because he has no consequence.

There are some kids, who when put in this situation, will try to please their dad because they would want their dad to be proud of them. But, given human nature, we know that most kids would try to get away with murder. What would happen if this child never got disciplined? Realistically, how much learning do you think that little boy would accumulate? As a child, his mind is not yet mature enough to grasp the reasoning of why these lessons are valuable. Not only will he fail, but he would corrupt the entire class in the process.

We have a principal that loves us enough to want us to have the best education possible so we have boundaries and rules. Our principal is the God and Goddess responsible for Creation in our portion of this Universe. The principal sees the bigger picture even if we don't.

So, let's switch our attention back to the lazy ancient human souls who instead of evolving past the third dimension kept repeating it because they had no motivation to move forward. This was stalling the process of the evolution of the souls. The system is set up to learn lessons in the third dimension of consciousness and move on to become co-creators in the fourth and fifth dimensions and so on.

Souls who have graduated to light-beings have the ability to create in other parts of other universes, thus taking on more and more roles in the Creator's ever-expanding multi-verses. Therefore, a decision was made to introduce a catalyst to motivate us. Duality and forgetfulness were added to the third-dimensional reality to help us grow. This act imported the concept of suffering into the world.

Suffering has been known to lead to peace and enlightenment faster than joy. We have all heard stories about how the most intense and powerful spiritual leaders emerged from the most twisted and tortured pasts. We all know someone who has spent an extended amount of time in prison and then gets out completely transformed and has "found God." Unfortunately for us, most of the time we have to touch the stove to see if it's hot. Our stubbornness is one of biggest downfalls, but at the same time, one of our greatest teachers.

People often wonder why God allows them to go through hard situations. There is a scripture text that says, "God never puts more on you than you can bear." It is so well known that it's become cliché. When suffering arises, we use this phrase as a coping mechanism to weather the storm. It will subconsciously be used as a strength gathering technique. It is an affirmation of victory in the face of adversity. There are, however, times that even the strongest man will doubt this verbiage.

When we have belief in an all-knowing, all-seeing God, we are more likely to believe that our lives are pre-planned for some kind of purpose and naively reject the notion that pain and hardships are pre-planned as well. We know that bad things happen to good people but the general consensus has been this is the work of evil. This denial has at some point caused suffering in all of us. The purpose of the spiritual path is to learn how to live in peace and harmony with everything around you, even in the midst of pain and suffering.

Some atheists scoff at the concept of an unconditional loving God and if you look at the situation logically, anyone can understand their point of view. How can a GOD love his Creation when we suffer the way we do? Why does God allow wars? Why do little kids die? Why does God allow sickness and suffering?

To not receive an answer these questions would understandably make a person turn his or her back on God. But maybe there is an answer. It is the same reason that a parent who is a school principal, will not save his son from a test or let him get out of doing his homework.

Our experiences are for a greater good. Each trauma and trial are a lesson. This is how we are supposed to learn so we can do better. We just don't get it because our society is still trying to control things out of fear. If we don't experience the bad, we won't know what good is. If we don't experience suffering, we will never know what joy is. We need grief to know happiness the same way we need winter to appreciate summer. This is part of the dualistic nature of our reality.

This is our classroom and we are the children who are sent here to learn. Just because the Creator doesn't intervene doesn't mean we are not being watched, protected and guided. The problem is that there are so many people running around fearing the unknown and trying to control what is uncontrollable, they become consumed with fear. When something unpleasant does happen, instead of us looking for the lesson or learning to focus on the silver lining in the gray cloud, we react with whatever raw emotion comes up first.

The thing that we fear the most is suffering and ninety-five percent of our energy is spent trying to relieve or avoid suffering. It is impossible to avoid everything we perceive as unpleasant. The suffering comes from the mind's perception but the truth is, if it happened, it was supposed to happen.

There are no accidents, mistakes or coincidences. Everything happens for a divine purpose. When we speak of God not being responsible for suffering this is yet another paradox. God ultimately created everything: matter, non-matter, light, spirit, waves, particles, ad infinitum, so technically sickness is still of God; however, there is a destiny to each of our lives, a beginning and an end that was orchestrated prior to our birth. It was orchestrated by our souls along with our teachers, guides, and the Creator. Sometimes it is ourselves who have previously decided we will deal with a particular ailment or problem to aide in our spiritual growth. This is called a contract. When we have a tie to a specific person that causes negative events; this is sometimes pre-planned as well. This is called a soul contract.

Therefore, God will allow what we deem as negative to plague us because of a pre-birth decision. This is where the term, "As above, so below," comes into play. In the Bible, Matthew 18:19, Jesus says, "Again I tell you this, if two of you agree on earth about anything you pray for, it will be done for you by My Father in heaven." (NLV) Divine Spirit is not uncaring.

We may feel alone, but we are not. We are sent here with angels, spirit guides, and our ancestors all helping us behind the scenes. Life is hard, but you knew that when you volunteered to come here. You were confident that you would succeed in mastering your lessons.

With knowing this mystical knowledge, we can now see why bad things happen to people. Once the veil of forgetfulness has been lowered our free will can allow for us to veer off of our predestined course at any time. The evolution of these new choices creates new outcomes and new models of reality. With 7 billion people making choices all at the same time, we are creating the reality we live in. We are the reason the world is the way it is. This is why a non-judgmental attitude is so important. The veil causes us to forget where and who we were before we got here, why we are here, and where we are headed when we die. A lot of times we do things out of plain old ignorance.

There are humans who have veered off course and then began a new course based on their free will decisions. They may engage in negative behavior and never find their way back on track. In their defense, spiritual knowledge is not the easiest principles to understand in today's time and age. If the soul doesn't know or learn how to access itself, he/she won't be able to see the effects of his/her actions until after his/her earthly transition. It is not for another soul to decide whether someone is good or bad, worthy or unworthy. Most of the time we are just ignorant, we just don't know.

There are times when the veil lifts just enough to give us hope needed to keep moving forward. Near death experiences, dreams, miracles, UFO sightings, and past life regressions are a few examples that provide us with more understanding and a knowing that there are supernatural powers at work that we can't explain. We must keep in mind that there is a reason for everything. Every event has purpose and potential for growth. That is one of the major reasons why we exist, to experience events in order to learn lessons.

Real Life Enlightenment   Part Two

-These Boots Were Made for Walking-

Walking the spiritual path is easier than it looks, to be honest. If you are earnestly searching for truth, you might find the process emotionally painful at first. The feeling of being alone in this world, being separate or even invisible to God is very gut-wrenching. The good news is the pain is only temporary and what waits on the other side more than makes up for it.

If you have made a decision to search for something deeper, it means you are fed up with superficial. You are tired of not understanding certain spiritual matters and being told not to question anything. You have to be rebellious and even a bit crazy to go down the road to spiritual awakening. For those who are hesitant to wade out into uncharted waters, you are not to blame. Observations from the outside can make spirituality or new age spiritual theories seem weird and confusing and make the people who practice them look like hippie crazed, crystal toting, meditating nut cases.

The most beneficial reason to give spirituality a try is so it can make your life better. There are human behaviors and theories that haven't produced satisfying results so far. If you take an honest, open look at the behavior of society as a whole, it seems to be getting worse with each passing year. Spirituality teaches us how to look at the world through clear and non-judgmental eyes. We forget that there are souls out here struggling to find their way just like we are.

The greatest ability gained by acquiring spiritual knowledge is the ability to love and accept self and love and accept others unconditionally. The golden rule is to treat people like you want to be treated and love people like you want to be loved. There is something that was left out of this declaration. You need to love self unconditionally before you can love others the same way.

You need to treat yourself the way you want others to treat you and love yourself the way you desire others to love you. This is one of the reasons why the divorce rate is so high. People are loving themselves partially and looking for others to fill in the rest of the love. You can't treat someone with positivity if you are consumed in negativity. If you are judgmental about self, you will be judgmental to those you love. If you mistreat and abuse self, you will naturally mistreat and abuse others. Most times, this is done so unconsciously that the individual soul is unaware of the mental self-inflicted abuse.

A spiritual path strengthens empathy, the ability to imagine oneself in someone else's shoes. Instead of condemning the lost soul, we should be more willing to show that person love, mercy and compassion. Getting to know the "I AM" on a deeper level will allow us to be a reflection of God's endless love. Feeling love instead of suffering is worth the journey...end of story.

Instead of suffering, we will know understanding and acceptance while following a more conscious spiritual path. We will always know that bad things will happen, but now, we will be able to replace negative unconscious reactions with deliberate conscious responses.

As we learn to become more aware of our emotions, choices and thought patterns, the path will help us change what we feel is not working for us. The majority of people think emotions cannot be controlled. This is an untrue statement. You cannot change someone else's behavior. You can influence them but you cannot change them. You can only change how you react.

Emotions are the part of the ego that helps process what's happening and categorizes it. Ego is a part of the mind, which is a part of the brain, which is a part of the body, which the spirit and soul animates. It is just a matter of putting the spirit and the soul in charge and taking control away from the ego. The soul/spirit, when used consciously, can have a great effect on the mind and even the body. This can be reached through understanding, awareness, practice, and meditation.

Awareness is the awakening from automatic and programmed thinking to a conscious focused, state of peace and love. It gets strengthened by intuition and Divinity's wisdom and grace and provides an understanding where there was none before. This new comprehension shows us what habits we have become accustomed to over the years, how to change our mindset and, in turn, change unwanted habits and behaviors.

There is a popular belief that habits are hard to break. We often say, "You can't teach old dog new tricks." Under the circumstances of a limited and misguided understanding, this cliché is very true. This is one of the reasons mistakes are repeated. To change a habit, you first have to change your mind. Then you develop a new mindset. After that, new behavioral patterns can replace old ones. You must find the root of the habit, analyze it and then make peace with it. Then all that is left is to consciously practice the new habit.

Take smoking, for example, there are a number of factors that keep addiction in charge of the action. There is the chemical dependency the body has on the product. We also cannot quit due to the physical actions of smoking called oral fixation: the act of holding the cigarette, bringing it to your lips, inhaling and exhaling. Lastly, we have a mental attachment in our brains and it tells us we need the cigarette.

We create rituals around smoking cigarettes. We have trained our brains to fetch and retrieve like dogs. Our inner mental alarm clock sounds at the appropriate times, after a meal, when we wake up, etc. If we cure the physical cravings without addressing the mental addiction the habit will never successfully be kicked. The brain will still be alarming, "We just ate, now we need a cigarette! We can't drink this beer without a cigarette!"

Even though we know good and well that diseases are directly related to smoking, most people still can't quit. People swear up and down that smoking helps them relax even though cigarettes lead to vasoconstriction of the blood vessels. In essence, your body is tensing up, not the other way around.

It's not even the cigarette that is relaxing, it's the deep breathing, the inhale-exhale that is relaxing the person. In order to quit, we have to find alternatives for all of the addiction. A nicotine patch alone isn't enough. We have to understand the purpose behind why we do the things we do.

-Eye Know Nothing-

We must learn to see reality as it really is. Today's reality is a matrix. It is a social construct based on societal archetypes. It has systems in place to keep things organized. Society also has ways of keeping the conditioning we are stuck in going strong. We have always functioned under these rules and never actively challenged the system to change. This system was here before you and I were here, and it will be here after you and I are gone.

This is the result of the evolution of humans. Being conscious allows us to re-evaluate situations and bring about change, even if it is personal change. Remember, every event has a catalyst attached to it. Every moment is an opportunity for growth. We own our individual consciousness and allow it to make decisions for us. There is a paradox to this. Free will is an illusion if you analyze it thoroughly. We are allowed to make choices throughout our life.

There are spiritual powers that won't intervene unless asked and still won't step in at times according to our predestined path. We assume that our choices determine where our soul will end up in the long run. The paradox is ALL roads lead back to the Creator. The human life we are living right now is just a tiny smidgen of what our soul has been and will go through. The human experience gets repeated by choice from the conscious decision of the soul while in the spirit world.

You may think someone that has been labeled as evil has separated himself from the Creator. They are in a state of being where their focus is not serving God or even serving mankind. Their priority is to serve self. Humans are the ones who judge this accordingly because of our built-in moral detector called a conscience.

We give a bad label to those who we feel lack good moral characteristics such as rapists, murderers, terrorists, and gays, and we feel in our own self-righteousness that they deserve to have eternal torture and damnation because they didn't adhere to the rules. What we don't realize is to go against your spiritual nature is already hell. The pull of God/love isn't easily ignored. We find fault with those who ignore this instinctual charge. We figure if we find this offensive, God will too. After all, we were created in his image, right?

The answer is yes, we were created in an image of love and light that came directly from the Creator's will into our being. We were also created with a free will that enables us to focus on other things besides this image. If you have ever wondered why there is war and poverty, see the previous sentence. We decide whether we suffer or not, have peace or troubled times, even condemn ourselves to a heaven or a hell.

However, the theory that all roads lead to God is so foreign to human existence and is not even explored for fear of losing control of the masses. There are some who are unable to associate an evil person with being a child of God. Their range of compassion, understanding and unconditional love just doesn't extend that far. There is a bigger picture of purpose that we are not able to see from our point of view. We are all God's children and our nature is to create. Whether we create chaos and confusion or order; love is up to us.

"Instead of thinking outside of the box, get rid of the box."

-Deepak Chopra-

-Maybe It's Not Maybelline-

Focusing our attention on our spiritual needs is imperative. We must exist with those people who have the free will to destroy the Earth if they see fit and it's hard to find happiness knowing that. Whether we believe in structured teaching or non-structured teaching we should follow whatever we feel in our hearts as our personal paths. Most spiritualists end up creating their own rituals based on the things they have learned but it doesn't always mean abandoning their core beliefs.

Spirituality gets judged as a place for rebels who have turned their backs on God but that isn't true. They have heard a different call and now they are trying to find out where it is coming from and what it wants them to do. If anything, the truth is they love God SO much that they simply want to obedient to their life's mission. You can't go down this road and not change. It isn't possible.

As we change and evolve on the inside, naturally, our outer appearance, our thinking, and our rituals will also change. We just must remember not to get caught up in clichés or pre-conceived notions of what being a spiritual person looks like. Honestly, the misconceptions about spirituality derive come from individual ideas about a misunderstanding. Society takes simple ideas and structures whole belief systems around them. We have gotten used to the fact that certain looks and behaviors come along with society's standard of being religious or spiritual.

These common standards create misgivings about having personal relationships with God. Spirituality is about growing in the Creator's love and light and uncovering hidden truth gems inside of ourselves. Trying to live up to nosebleed high standards is the quickest way to fail at reaching personal spiritual goals. The problem is when we look at someone from the outside we don't see the problems they go through and the journey they have been on. Even the most spiritually-minded persons have struggles from time to time.

We can't get caught up in the illusion of what being spiritual is supposed to look like. If we do that, we end up with a bunch of people who look the part on the outside but are mentally dying on the inside. Before we can begin to grow we should be completely honest with God, then ourselves. One thing is for sure, no matter how perfect we might look on the outside EVERYBODY has issues.

Ego creates a lot of problems when left unchecked and underdeveloped. The chakra system in some people have lower levels that might be active but the higher realms might remain dormant. That is the reason why sometimes someone can love God and want to serve and obey God but is unable to live up to their social standards of obedience to God.

Matthew 26:41 explains this: the spirit is willing but the flesh is weak. It is true that the ego/flesh is weak and has to die daily like the Bible says. This only means we should keep the ego in check and in balance. Practicing the art of acceptance and surrender before action will help curb illogical and unnecessary emotional impulses. However, this whole, "I must look a certain way to impress God," idea is misdirected. If God is an unconditional loving deity you have to know that the rules that are placed on certain spiritual processes are for our own benefits, not God's. ALL OF the THEM...the worship, the praise, the rituals...they are for OUR benefits, not Divinity's. They are in place to help us grow.

As we strive to become better people we must realize that is really not as serious as we make it out to be. Adversity is a part of life and it is the challenges that make life worthwhile. Without adversities, life would be boring. We start off with a goal, work towards it, accomplish it and we feel that feeling of elation that makes all the work worth it…. then we set another goal. That pretty much sums up our life in a nutshell. There are spiritualists who feel like they need to portray an image that is synonymous with "looking spiritual." There is no such thing. Someone who looks the part can be far from their goals and someone who looks like a regular "Joe" can be an enlightened being.

We must remember, individuals come in all different shapes, sizes, colors, and lifestyles. We all have different physical and personality traits. We, as humans, should be allowed to experience and explore aspects of life without judgment from each other. God loves us for who we are. Every experience on earth is a learning experience. There is no such thing as an accident or a mistake. The bottom line is people learn in different ways and progress at various degrees. There is no reason for a conservative Christian, for example, to judge a punk rock atheist because the atheist is God's child too. And God lets him be who he is. Why can't we?

There are many roads that lead to union with God and many methods of understanding God. Some use religion, philosophy, math, science, history and even nature to connect with the Most High. All roads lead to God. Eventually, we will ALL get it and see the light, even if it isn't in this lifetime. We all know that Hitler was one of the few humans that was near-universally despised for his deeds by other humans. Yes, even his soul's road will eventually even lead him to God. That's hope. Hopefully, this will give you comfort if you think you've fucked it all up thus far. For those who feel that their purpose is helping or teaching God's children to love and understand themselves, there is nothing wrong with that path either, even if all we end up doing is regurgitating someone else's beliefs or theories.

To persuade an individual to accept a truth is a good thing, but we can't shove what we believe down someone else's throat and then get mad when they do not want to hear it. Since perception is personal we cannot take it personally when our personal truth isn't accepted by others. It is not our job to convince others that our truth is the right one. We can offer it and then trust the Supreme Source to take care of that person's spiritual needs.

We are just like the waiter that serves food that the chef prepares. It is not the waiter's job to convince the patron to eat the food. It is the waiter's job to present the food and that is all. If the customer discards the meal without even tasting it, it should be of no concern to the waiter. In truth, that is the chef's concern. It's not about right or wrong. It's about intention. It's about what is in your heart.

People focus so much on what is on the outside. There is absolutely nothing wrong with adorning the body for strictly the pleasure of it. Human nature, naturally, has us focused on the five senses because we use them to navigate through life. We are visual creatures because vision makes the illusion real to us. But when your entire existence depends on how you look on the outside, your life is going to suck every time you have a bad hair day. Putting lipstick on your lips will not change the mess that is buried deep inside. Polishing the outside of our bodies only distracts; it doesn't help solve the problem. The crap that we sweep under the rug never disappears. It is there, and we see it every time we take a peek under the rug.

Part Three

-Tightrope Walker-

The process of learning is slow and tedious. Imagine if the spiritual path is a tightrope. You are a circus performer learning how to master the tightrope. There is only one problem: you are afraid of heights. The directions you are receiving from the instructor seem confusing and frightening. You don't even know why you signed up in the first place, but it is too late to back down. In the beginning, of course, you will be wobbly and fall at the slightest sense of uncertainty. As a matter of fact, the rope is no more than an inch off of the ground after an extended amount of practice. You haven't even seen any tangible progress.

The thought of quitting keeps circling around in your mind and you don't have a lot a confidence that you'll actually be able to pull this off. Your emotions are all over the place ranging from sadness, anger, and frustration when you are not getting it, to determination, pride and joy when you can actually see your skills of tightrope walking growing. You started off with having the rope on the ground and slowly, that rope is inched higher into the air. You learn how to balance yourself and steady yourself with practice. The higher that rope raises off of the ground, the surer of yourself you become.

The crazy part is, if your emotions weren't all over the place you would have mastered the beginning stages at a faster rate. These out-of-control emotions stem from fear, a fear of heights, fear of falling, fear of the unknown, fear of being hurt and so on. Fear is at the root of every negative emotion ever conceived. Fear causes spiritual stagnation, and struggle. Fear cause us not to want to pursue anything new. It hinders our experiences. Regardless of how badly we would want to tightrope walk, fear will keep us on the ground forever.

We can and should learn to embrace something foreign without fear. The mastery of a new skill can bring so much joy. It might start off slow, but if you continue with it and don't give up, you will get where you imagined. The same thing applies to our spiritual journey. It is scary and uncertain in the beginning and what's even worse is the instructor can't be seen with the naked eye. You will have setbacks, possible injuries, and doubtful moments. Sometimes all you can do is press on to fulfill the goals you set out to accomplish.

You WILL eventually rise further and further off the ground. You may need a safety net at first but if you stick to it, you can eventually get rid of any crutches. You will do it. You are doing it. You are walking that tightrope. Look, ma, no hands! Your spiritual journey will take you to unknown heights. Instead of fear, you will have exhilaration. All you have to do in order to learn from the Creator is be open to learning. That's it.

The truth is: life's a journey, not a destination. It is in our nature, as humans, to continue to create even after we have reached previous set goals. Nothing is satisfying for long because our contentment changes to boredom very easily. We always want more. When we set a goal and then achieve it, all we do afterward is set another goal and work towards achieving that goal. This is the image we were created in. We were made by a creator to continue the evolution of Creation.

We will all agree that there are moments where life seems hard. The reason the word "seems" is used is because we rate the level of difficulty based on our perception of what "hard" is. If we change our perception we can and will change our point of view and our reactions. Life is only hard because we choose to believe that it is hard. Our belief creates thought and thought is a vibration. What we put out, we get back. The vibration creates our reality. If we think it is hard, hard, hard, we'll just get more of that. This goes for any other conclusion we come to. If we walk around saying, "I'm always broke" it is guaranteed we will stay broke. "As a man thinketh, so is he." It's right there in the Bible.

The thought process invokes the reality laid out. You have to stop the cycle of negative thinking and get off of the merry-go-round of frustration and doubt. How do we do that? Don't feed into what you see. What you see does not have to be acknowledged. It's almost like following the old cliché "fake it until you make it." You can focus on what you want until you get it.

You can proclaim that you are rich even if you are still financially struggling. You can proclaim you have good health even though the body may be battling an illness. This takes practice, however, because most people are quick to complain about how sucky they feel. Venting and being honest are cool but don't believe that what you see can't change. Instead of saying, "I'm sick," we should change that to, "I'm looking forward to feeling better and I am grateful to be alive." This wording changes our focus to gratitude and speaks better days into existence at the same time.

Life is the teacher and we are constant students. We change, we grow, and we deal with the different events as they unfold. Life can be as hard or as easy as you think it is. Imagine being in a peaceful state no matter what is going on in life. Impossible? No, absolutely not. It would be for someone who already relishes in their failure instead of focuses on their success. When you unlock the limits of your potential, anything is possible. It is all based on how you look at it. So, imagine being hopeful that you can achieve a state of inner peace. Would it fall right into place? Perhaps. The mind would have to be reprogrammed and it takes concentration, focus, and practice. The spiritual concepts are actually simple, it is our minds that are already programmed to believe the worst. You have to realize what you know, what doesn't fit and reprogram it. You must learn a new way to think before you can master a new way to be.

You can start out as a player on a team with other players, a coach, referees and an audience. You can end up knowing you control the game and all aspects of the game. It is you who decides what game you want to play, and how you want to play it. All of the playbooks for all of the games are stored in your spiritual DNA. All you have to do is get over the fear that you are incomplete, insufficient, and incapable. God made all things perfect, complete, limitless just like God herself. We are a mirror as well.

-The Dark Night of The Soul-

Ok, so now you have decided to give in to this yearning for truth. What happens next? Usually chaos. To step out on faith and seek spiritual truth is called a "declaration". No matter how strong and determined the declaration is, it is a very scary position to be in. Everything we have learned in the past and came to regard as truth will have to be questioned. Everything isn't certain anymore. Emotionally, this comes with a certain level of anxiety. Spiritualists call this the dark night of the soul. It is different for each individual but some commonalities are anxiety, fear, uncertainty, and depression. It is a considered by some a negative experience but it is just the storm before the rainbow.

Some people feel as though God has abandoned them. It feels lonely. You will feel alone. It's mighty breezy out there on that limb by yourself. The dark night of the soul represents the amount of time a soul feels lost at the beginning of the spiritual path. It varies from person to person and it doesn't always occur. It is characterized by feelings of questioning, loss, mourning, frustration, and confusion. Mental and spiritual suffering is not uncommon. There is a sense of fear of the unknown present. We question the direction of the path or lack thereof. It feels like you are alone in the world. You feel regretful and some people even pedal backward. It is not uncommon to re-enter whatever belief or non-belief structure that was previously abandoned.

The dark night of the soul is what happens after you challenge everything you have been taught or think should be true. Our brains fight to hold on to the illusion, even though we know we want something real. Once we can see the true reality instead of what we want to see, there is a period of adjustment we must go through. Our thoughts and beliefs are not only held in our brain but in every cell and organ in our body. Several belief systems are often tied to one thought or illusion. The breakdown of these illusions can be traumatizing to the body and to our emotional state. We experience a grieving and a loss for the comfort of our illusions. We step into the unknown.

The dark night of the soul represents classic fear of the unknown. Fear is a pre-programmed instinct to ensure our survival. To be afraid when exploring things of a spiritual nature is a downright traumatic experience. This condition goes along with a universal law of cause and effect. When making any type of declaration to the universe, the opposite is going to happen. This is the test that comes after the lesson.

We know this as "Murphy's law" but this is the nature of reality. In our dualistic existence, catalysts are always present to motivate choice and ultimately growth. When you make a statement saying something like, "I am going to walk in my truth or I want to know the truth about God" you are going to immediately get the opposite; fear and self-doubt. When you make a declaration, you get a test. The dark night of the soul is the test. You want spiritual truth but are you ready for spiritual truth? The dark night of the soul definitely prepares you if you are not ready.

Fortunately, it is temporary and begins to subside when the will of the soul focuses on finding its hidden truth and has faith in God/Universe to provide us with what we need. You must face yourself in the eyes of your God, question your own worthiness and your integrity. You are faced with a mirror. You are alone in this. There is no one there but you and God. The dark night of the soul feels like a punishment but it's not. It's more like a refiner's fire. You have to heat metals at extremely hot temperatures in order to mold the precious stones into valuable objects. The fire also cleans debris off of it. We must go through the same process with our diamond/soul.

Our diamond/soul from the earlier analogy is the most precious gift we have. Diamonds are often found deep in caves and covered by dirt, dust, and rock. Along the same lines, our diamond souls are covered by ego, traumatic experiences, grief, anger, mistakes and fear. We, as truth seekers, must go through the process of cleaning off our diamond souls. This can be very tasking considering all the grit and grime that has built up over the years.

This is why the dark night of the soul dives head first into where the most crap is buried. Some advice would be to stand strong in the face of doubt. Know you are not alone and this is a normal phenomenon. It is impossible for the God to leave our side because the Spirit of God permeates everything. It might seem lonesome but there are others who have gone through this before you and will go through this behind you. It is a rite of passage to spiritual truth and freedom. It will pass, just as everything else is temporary.

-The Wilderness Experience -

The wilderness experience immediately follows the Declaration and the Dark Night of the Soul. Its name comes the Bible story in the book of Exodus about the children of Israel. They wandered in the wilderness for forty years before entering the promised land of Canaan.

This is not the same as the Dark Night. This is the "Ask and you shall receive" part. You asked for the truth and you will get it. It can come from anyone, anywhere and at any time. A whirlwind of information will begin to come from all directions, even from unlikely sources. The trick is to pay attention, be open to the information and follow your heart's guidance...that's it. But of course, we humans, like to analyze things and put our own little cute labels on things. We just try to make sense of what is happening to us.

The only true purpose for spreading spiritual material is to provide somewhat of a map to a generalized location. There is no specific map with an "X" marking the treasure. It is more like a nod in a general direction. Ultimately, what compels people to actively engage a spiritual path is the pursuit of happiness and peace. The whole process, if done correctly, will teach us that happiness, joy, and peace are not something on the outside to be attained, but that it is and always has been right here on the inside. We go through this whole song and dance just to find out we are searching for what was never lost.

In our society, it is common to look for love and happiness in our relationships, our accomplishments, our social statuses, our money or our material possessions. All of that is truly pointless because it will never fill the void for long.

In order for you to find the answers, you must look within. The biggest oxymoron happens when we look outside of ourselves for answers that are buried deep inside of us. Society's concepts are backwards. It teaches joy and happiness are found in success and prosperity. These will bring happiness but it is not a lasting happiness. The peace that Jesus had while in the midst of the storm looks as if it is impossible to attain but it is found by knowing who you really are. You are a powerful, spiritual being who is enjoying the privilege of co-creating your reality alongside your Creator. When you walk in absolute truth you begin to grow in the confidence of what you can do. You realize then that boundaries are make-believe. They do not really exist.

The illusion of separateness is only there to enhance spiritual growth, but, nevertheless, it is an illusion. In truth, we are all connected and live on this earth together. We are connected to Mother Earth, as a living entity that we dwell upon. We are connected to each other physically, emotionally, spiritually and anatomically. Our job, while we are here, is to grow spiritually, love
each other and ourselves unconditionally, and fulfill our purpose for coming here in the first place.

There are a lot of paths crossing which intersects our souls with other souls' journeys. We collide and intermingle and view events and reactions from our own personal perspective. However, we feel separate and because we feel separate; we cannot feel the all-inclusiveness.

Being in a body appears to cut us off from the outside world. It houses our personal thoughts, personal memories, feelings, and even causes us to feel and know things that our senses pick up on when others around us might not feel the same vibes. This allows for us to have a unique experience while we are here. It gives us personal perception and perspective. This allows for uniqueness in every human. Even though we are all unique we are still united in Love because we are products from the Source of All. We make up a collective consciousness of the human existence.

Life's lessons are about growing, of course, but at the same time, they are gifts to be cherished, enjoyed and lived out to the highest degree as possible. More often than not, we fall short of the latter goals. Simply put, we should start each day off with gratitude and have the mind frame of, "Follow your bliss." Do what makes your heart sing, follow your dreams, laugh and love as much as possible. There is nothing wrong with striving for perfection but if it is because you want God to love and accept you, please understand that God already loves and accepts each one of us. Accept and love yourself and there is nothing wrong with reaching for righteousness at the same time.

Spirituality is not about taking away, but it is about adding to the spiritual foundation you already have. It is not about taking anything away from your own individual personality. It is about getting you to realize that your spirit is much more powerful than your ego or personality. There are some religious lifestyles that have specific rules and consequences for breaking their rules. Spirituality teaches the individual to search their own heart and spirit and do what is right for them.

Aligning one's true nature with one's spiritual purpose will create never-ending bliss here on earth. The spirit already holds all the answers, it is just waiting for the soul to get with the program, and the personality to stop feeding into the pre-programmed merry-go-round of the ego.

Yes, there is a need for rules, don't get me wrong. Being spiritual doesn't mean you can just go out and do whatever you want. The universe is built based on laws, but truth is always based on perception and perception is aided by experience. Even if we don't consciously remember how a certain fact got stored in our mental rolodex as truth, we identify with those strong feelings of "this is right" when we feel them.

The key to understanding new spiritual information is to use the sense that is so rarely used, the sixth sense. We call it by many different names. Some names are the Holy Spirit, instinct, intuition, our first mind, our gut feeling and the list goes on…

We have a built-in "bullshit" detector. Liken your flow of information to a beautiful ballad being played on a piano. Every time we receive a message that doesn't match our personal vibration, it will feel like that beautiful piano ballad just hit a wrong note. Our ability to notice what we have dubbed, "red flags," is a crucial element on the path. We just have to remember to keep it personal. Our instructional knowledge might not necessarily be meant for someone else.

There is a phrase that says, "Chew the fish and spit out the bones." This means take and utilize what you need and ignore what you don't. Fish is going to have bones sometimes; meaning there are truths and untruths in every situation. Every religion has flaws. Every piece of spiritual information has flaws because it is filtered through the human experience which is designed to be flawed. Every knowledgeable point made in this book is not going to resonate with every single person who reads it. Take the information you need and don't worry about the information you don't need. Knowing "self" is to know what you need and what works for you.

For example, what bothers one person might not bother another. Some people like roller coasters, some people hate horror movies. The longer we are on this planet, the more we should know what motivates and moves us as individuals. We should use the information and accept ourselves instead of pretending to be things we are not. You have to accept a negative situation as being what it is

Real Life Enlightenment   Part Three

before you can work to make it better. Honesty makes the process so much faster although it can be more painful. Pain and suffering is the best way to learn our lessons. It's unfortunate but true. At least you know you are not the only one going through it.

You can say to someone, "Don't touch the stove, it's hot. Don't touch the stove, it's hot. It will burn you and you will be in pain." But we can never fully understand the magnitude of what "hot" is unless we touch the stove. We have to feel those pain sensors sending a domino effect through our nervous system, up to the brain, having the brain register and process the impulses and then we feel the actual pain.

There is nothing like feeling it yourself because then you know, without a shadow of a doubt, what it feels like to have the pain. Bet you won't touch that stove ever again...or maybe, you will. But there is no foolproof way to avoid pain. You know the stove is hot, but one day you are going to be taking a pot off the stove and you are going to get burned. It is no avoiding it. You can be as careful as you can, but accidents happen. We try to avoid mental pain even more than we avoid physical pain.

The ego receives our mental pain receptors and processes them. The ego is our guard dog but it sometimes gets overzealous. It wants to avoid the pain at all costs. The problem is the ego doesn't accept that pain is a part of life so it uses our emotions as a pain buffer. That never works because emotions are pain receptors, not buffers. Do not let ego pull you into a pain circle. When you don't learn from your mistakes you will repeat them. That is a universal law. The pain comes with the lesson. Don't focus on the pain, focus on learning the lesson. What did this painful experience teach you? What did you learn???

99 | P a g e

-The Broccoli or The Burger-

It is crucial that you understand your true nature and how this whole mind, body and spirit thing works. These gifts were given to you. It is our responsibility to take care of them. We might as well figure out how to use them to the fullest capacity. The cliché, "You are what you eat," made famous by nutritionist Victor Lindlahr goes further than just talking about the food we take in. It encompasses what we feed our mind and soul as well.

What we desire and reflect, we get back. What we observe, we ingest. What we subject ourselves to can either enhance our growth or inhibit our growth, even on something as small as a vibratory scale. There are a few strong things that can quickly raise or lower our vibrations. One of the biggest influences is music. A musical instrument literally produces vibration. This is why some religious groups discourage listening to any other music than that religion's music. They know that music can influence the mood or the heart of the person. They try to remove this potential exposure to negativity to protect the integrity of the soul.

Music is one of the most powerful tools there is to aid in increasing and maintaining positive vibrations. It has the ability to anchor an emotion or an event to us. You can still recall that hot summer song in 1993 if it came on. Not only do you remember what you were doing but you remember where you were in life, emotionally, that year. Your recall takes you right back to that moment in time. We pay attention to how the song makes us feel. We pay attention to how everything makes us feel although it happens so quickly we don't usually notice. Our sub-conscious is being influenced by our surroundings at all times.

Laughter, nature, music, meditation, people, places or things that hold good vibes are tools we can use to raise our spiritual vibrations. Emotions are contagious so we should be careful around certain people. Have you ever been in a good mood and ran into someone who was upset? Then, they tell you what's wrong and the next thing you know, you're upset? Everything exists on a vibratory level and this is an example of that. The scientific rationale behind this phrase is the "vibrating atoms" theory mentioned earlier. But the lesser known theory is these vibrations carry energy patterns. More bluntly put, people, places, and things carry vibes. Some people can feel the emotional vibration in things, some other people can feel emotional vibrations more in places, but most of us feel it off of other people.

You are what you eat, meaning your soul is whatever you feed it. This is hard because we live in a world where modern society is full of stimuli with low vibrations attached to it. Sex, drugs, and violence dominate our external stimuli and affect our internal mindset. We have all felt bad vibes before. And we have all been in situations where we haven't trusted our gut instincts. This instinct is the sixth sense that doesn't get developed enough. This is the Holy Spirit and we usually ignore it during daily life. When we aren't consciously aware of the energy vibrations that are in our surroundings, we become susceptible to them.

"Energy is neither created nor destroyed but is transferred from one form to another," quoted a wise man. We are energy. We must be aware of what we expose our energy to. The mind is fed and fueled by outside stimuli and inner thoughts. Remember, the Bible says, "As a man thinketh, so is he." This is so important that it bears repeating. This means your thoughts create your reality. The outer stimuli that you expose yourself to help to determine the course of your inner thoughts. If you are thinking negative, you will attract negative situations. If you are thinking positive you will attract positive situations. You cannot do something like participate in gossip and then say you don't like drama. You are creating the conditions for drama to arise. You cannot say "I want to lose weight" and then continue to keep the same eating habits. You will stay fat.

If you want to change, you have to do the work. You have to move beyond the declaration. The spirit is born hidden behind a veil of forgetfulness. You have forgotten who you really are and what you are doing here. It is your job to remember. It is more than your job. It is your right. It is your key to freedom.

Just like a car, if you take care of it, change the oil regularly, get tune-ups, etc., you will have a better chance of smoother running vehicle. The same goes for the trinity of mind, body, and spirit. We pay attention to the body part out of the three but not the mind and spirit. Firstly, you have to take time out in order to observe what you feed your mind. You cannot keep peace of mind if you feed it negativity. This includes violence, confusion and other negative things. Certain things will no longer serve your needs as you expand your mind and spirit. You can try, but as you grow, the universe will send you things to reflect your growth. You can't want better and do the same things. We have to elevate our frequencies.

The human body also responds to the frequency of its intake. Everything around us, including food, has its own vibrational frequency. What we ingest, based on its own frequency, can either elevate our body's frequency or lower our body's frequency. Natural fruits and vegetables have higher vibrational frequencies than processed foods, meats, sugary products, and fried foods. We see the results of this process daily. If you feed the body a bunch of garbage, you will end up obese and disease stricken. This is the blunt truth. Food's purpose is to provide the body with energy. The more efficient the fuel, the better the results. We, in modern day society, do not pay attention to what we put in our bodies. We have been conditioned to do what everyone else is doing.

Our society has been seduced by quick and easy food preparation so we end up not paying attention to the fact that those processed meals and foreign chemicals are having negative effects on our bodies. We deal with headaches, migraines, constipation, and indigestion among other things and never once think that perhaps, we are causing our own problems. What we eat can send us into a world of disease and medical problems but our minds have been trained to ignore these facts. In modern society, food consumption has morphed from a survival experience to a pleasure experience.

We want to eat what tastes good, but we all know the most delicious foods have the worst nutritional benefits. We develop diseases due to lack of a decent diet and regular exercise and then depend on prescriptions medicine to give us the magic cure. We have no discipline and very little self-control. It is our God-given right to eat whatever we want to at the end of the day; however, self-love should be included with our self-care.

This body is a gift to us in this lifetime. Good nourishment should be a form of appreciation for this gift. But, the body is not the only thing to be balanced. The mind and the spirit need attention and nurturing, as well.

Balance is extremely important. In order to achieve a place of constant inner peace, you must understand the true Trinity. In this context, the trinity means the mind, the body and the spirit. According to sources about Chakra activation, it is understood that it doesn't matter how open the chakras are, what matters is that they are balanced. And so, it is our duty to balance our divine trinity.

Too much of ANYTHING is not good. Most people take that and apply it to sex, drugs and bad foods but it is not limited to just those things. You can, also, apply it to books, meditation, and even leafy, green vegetables. To prove my point, we know that eating too many carbs and not enough protein can throw the body off balance. So, if you only eat fruits and not vegetables, even though fruit is healthy, you can still cause damage to your body. Addiction can be caused by doing anything in excess until it becomes a habit. This can damage the body's energy system.

A health nut will not be able to relate to an obese person, even though they are more alike than the health nut realizes. Neither will see the similarities because they are too busy looking at the differences on the outside. The truth is that they are both taking things to an extreme. Likewise, if you look at one who meditates all day and has gotten skilled at maintaining their own world of peace, sometimes you might see them react with an intolerable attitude to one who is still struggling to walk a righteous and spiritual path. They are still missing the point because they have taken things to an extreme. You need balance.

One who swims in the ocean, constantly, may love the water and never want to go back to the beach. However, it is necessary to get out of the water every once in a while. To ignore this will be detrimental to the body. The ocean water will wreak havoc on the skin: wrinkling it, making it itch and so on. The desire for food and drink will gradually escalate causing conflict to set in. The water temperature will drop, the body will become weary and even though the love for the ocean never fades, self-preservation will win out. You MUST get out of the ocean at some point.

The following sections of this book will begin to provide tools to strengthen the mind and spirit. The body's rules of well-being are well known in the knowledge of nutrition. The mind and the spirit? not so much....

-Scaredy Cat -

We have reviewed fear in previous sections. So now that we know how it shows up in our lives, the next question is, "How do you overcome fear?" The answer is deal with it. Face it. Over and over if you have to. Stand up to it, do not run. Of course, we don't want to deal with it because we don't like the feeling, but we must. Fear stands in between us and freedom. We cannot shortcut this process. There is a proverb that says, "The road to hell is wide and paved with good intentions." This means you don't have to be a bad person to end up in a bad situation. Sometimes, trying to take the easy way out only makes it worse.

Running from suffering only causes more suffering. Yes, suffering can be used as a catalyst for growth but we still need balance. Too much suffering just causes traumatization. You can never achieve oneness and truly be at peace as long as daily operation comes from a place of fear. Fear is something that is going to constantly show up over and over again, for the rest of your life. It settles inside of you and creates what is called a "pain body" or pain "shadow." A pain body is the sum total of painful experiences that you have collected in your psyche that becomes this negative recurrent energy. It brings along with it suffering, anxiety, and fear.

The more you feed the pain body, the more it grows. It can overwhelm your thought processes at the time of tribulation and swallow you in a sea of anguish. We know it by its many more familiar names such as mental illness and depression. You can overcome it by facing your fears, standing in your truth and accepting and loving yourself for who you are. We will never fully eliminate fear because it is pre-programmed. There are some people who have battled this monster for so long that they have lost the hope for victory. That is ok, too. It is never a person's fault that they deal with mental illness or other ailments. Doing your best sometimes simply means making it through the day. Just do your best.

Embrace the things you have been hiding, the things you don't want people to know about you, the thing you have been ashamed of and embarrassed to admit existed. By embracing your flaws, you can heal your pain body. Meditation and lifting your inner vibrations can also assist in dissolving the pain body. It is very important that you find and maintain a support system. You need someone to talk to in rough times.

Talking discharges the energy you would normally internalize and use to feed the pain body. Recognizing bad habits and unwanted behavior patterns is half the battle to defeating them. Don't be so hard on yourself. Focus on the positive instead of the negative. Visualizing success and reflecting the goals that have already been met will encourage and motivate you to do better. Dancing, singing, listening to inspiring music, yoga, painting, art, and hobbies all are known to raise your body's spiritual vibrations.

The purpose of seeking higher vibrations is to not succumb to the depression and despair that comes along with the ups and downs of everyday life. No matter how much we may try to be in control, things are going to happen that are out of our control, therefore, we need healthy coping mechanisms. Despair leads to all types of negative reactions in the body. It leads to mental illness and even physical sickness. It leads to hopelessness. To be hopeless is to believe a personal or non-personal situation will never change. It is the opposite of faith. Being hopeless guarantees for a hopeless situation because low mental vibrations will repel any attempts at positivity. This is the law of attraction. You will be stuck in a cycle of sadness and fear. You will not be living life, you will just be existing. To quote George Gurdjieff:

"Self-observation brings a man to the realization of the necessity of self-change. And in observing himself a man notices that self-observation itself brings out certain changes in his inner processes. He begins to understand that self-observation is an instrument of self-change, a means of awakening."

In order to move to a place from low mental vibration and break the cycle, we must use what is already in our arsenal, our brains. We can use our conscious mind to bring us to a better state of awareness. The "Reflective Thought technique" moves us out of an unconscious reflex action and into a more planned, deliberate response. This technique was birthed during my own spiritual journey. Here's how it works. Upon waking up in the morning, remind yourself to pay attention to every situation that plays itself out throughout the day.

Go throughout your regular day, then at night, before bed, devote time to reflect on the day's events. Mentally, take note of how you reacted to the events of the day. Assess your feelings in those moments of daily living and notice how you reacted to those unplanned situations that popped up. Decide if you agree with how you handled the situations. Visualize how would have reacted as a better version of yourself.

Pay attention to yourself more than anyone else does. What type of person are you? What type of person do you want to be? Do these enough times and you will find yourself, catching yourself before you react. You will have created a gap in between awareness and ego. This space is what is needed for you to walk in the power of your own free will. You will have broken the power of the unconscious mind.

Stress management is important as well, for raising vibrations. You can't just identify the stressors, you must identify and manage the coping mechanisms. You need to replace unhealthy coping mechanisms with healthier ones. Attachment to objects exaggerates and distorts reality and cause a great deal of stress. You don't really own anything anyway. Nothing belongs to you. When you die the bank will take your house back...or your kids will sell it...or their kids will sell it. Your kids will grow up to be their own individuals. Everything you depend on to make you happy and everything that you love is temporary...including your own body.

Learn how to simply be happy without things or people. Depend on no one else but yourself for your own happiness and hold no one accountable for your happiness but yourself. Anger destroys peace of mind. It is not even necessary most of the time. Pride breeds anger and is also unnecessary. You may have been able to change certain situations because you displayed anger but I bet, nine times out of ten, that same event keeps repeating itself in your life.

Ignorance is at the root of all delusion. Educate yourself. Don't be afraid to admit something you don't know. Believe in yourself and know you can always simply change your mind. You don't have to be stuck to one view and one opinion. That is why you were given free will. You can always change your mind.

How to Train Your Dragon

In the above phrase, the "dragon" represents the ego. Yes, the ego can be trained. If not, it will be like a stray dog running wild in the street and causing nothing but problems for you. It is yours, it belongs to you, it can do as you say. First, you have to separate your awareness from your ego (identity). Do this by paying attention to inner dialogue. Next, analyze the patterns of your thoughts. Recognize what it is and become aware of what it is doing. Be truthful about you to yourself. You are not your bad habits. You are not your negative personality. It is separate from you. You are awareness. You are the something that is aware and watching these thoughts and emotions. Don't act like you haven't watched yourself act a damn fool and wonder the next day, "Why did I do that?" We have all had those moments where we have lost control. The bigger question is if we lost control who did we give it to? Hmm.

Our first instinct might be to push the memory of this deep down in our minds, bury it as quickly as possible and pretend that it never happened. We do this because of guilt, shame, embarrassment, and fear of judgment from others. The worst thing we could do to ourselves is to hide it. We need to embrace it as part of ourselves and love ourselves as a whole. Work on it, of course, but accept it. Pay attention to things that happen and ask yourself why do you react the way you do?

Do not ask why the situations happen in the first place because if you do, that will only lead to finger pointing and blame. That is a pointless mission because, in life, shit happens, and shit is going to happen whether you want it to or not. The more open and honest we are with ourselves the more spiritual growth can take place. The analyzing exercise of self-reflection can continue for however long you need to do it. Self-growth should be a daily process. Remember, we are not always going to get it right. In order to make a good omelet, you have to break a few eggs. There will be bad days but you will change for the better if you keep at it.

The truth is, "there is no spoon." To quote a line from The Matrix. Do not try to bend the spoon, that's impossible. There is no good day or bad day. The day is whatever you make it, regardless of what happens. This concept is foreign to most of us because we are used to getting into situations and reacting unconsciously to them. Our ego and emotions are used to process information and participate in the outward world. When you identify with being your ego or your emotions, you will suffer greatly.

Anguish comes from the double edge sword of the ego. The ego is silently telling you: you are not doing things right. It is just as critical of you as it is of everything else. That little sucker is very tricky and will suck you into the games that it plays. Once you understand this is something that belongs to you and is not "you" it makes you feel a lot better in the long run. Try to refrain from judging yourself when you observe a negative behavior you display. It will take time to break it. Nothing happens overnight.

You have the power to replace bad thoughts with conscious good thoughts. All it takes is practice. The truth is that emotions can be controlled. Undesirable behaviors can be corrected. Have you ever heard somebody say, "I am too old to change?" Even though it is another society accepted cliché, what they are really saying is, "It is really hard to change and I am too tired to try. I would rather just be set in my ways." Any thought process can be corrected with consciously trained focus. Universal law says change is inevitable. Evolution is a naturally occurring process. Society as whole moves from one thought process to another and as long as the majority are dictating and engaging in the concept it will be approved regardless of rationality or moral decency.

The word "can't" is an extremely powerful word. As a matter of fact, all words are powerful. Most of us just aren't careful as to how we use them. We toss around the word "can't" and increase our resistance to things. We feel helpless and truly believe that seemingly hard situations are impossible to get past. We are just used to reacting aimlessly and that makes us feel out of control. Have you ever heard someone give a reason for some negative or irrational action and they say, "I am only human?" Or "I can't help it." Or "I can't control who I love."

Even if a person knows they are wrong they will still try and use one of this tired, vapid expressions. When you are used to just reacting and not using your conscious brain these responses are true. We *are* human. We all make mistakes, but where we mess up is using these above statements to dismiss an action and not analyzing what occurred. There is no "why did I do that?" or "What is going on with me to make me react like that?" There is no exploration. There is no accountability. Why should there be? Everyone around us makes these excuses. Everyone reacts based on their emotions.

Emotions are split-second shooters. They shoot from the hip first and ask questions later. The brain is a quick draw, and then before you know it the person on the receiving end of that verbal or physical bullet is catching hell. We are subliminally taught that we cannot control our emotions by what we see. So, of course, if we believe we can't control them.... we can't control them. Unfortunately, man assumes that since he can't control his emotions, God probably can't either. Since we are made in the image of God, he must have just as many issues as we have. God is known as a loving God, but also a jealous God, a vengeful God, and a God who is judgmental. A judgment from an unconditionally loving God is contradictory. Humans are known to behave in an irrational state at times. It's no wonder this behavior is observed in our personified image of God.

The human mind is one of the least understood subjects in the scientific world. We don't even know where consciousness originates in the brain. Science will dismiss an NDE as a mental hallucination, but cannot tell you why the mind sends these visions involuntarily when near death. Yes, we are human. To be only human means we are our bodies, our thoughts, and we are reacting on impulse and instinct. Most people think that is the extent of being human but it's not. To be a human "being" is to accept who and what you really are. It is accepting we have the power to transcend stress and suffering. It is walking in the truth that every event, thought, feeling, particle, everything is of God. When you see in that, you sit in peace, truth, and love. You sit in what God really is. Just the same, when you sit in negativity, despair, and depression this is also of God. It's just a matter of which angle you want your perspective to face.

The surrender to the flow of life kills the ego. This means you accept things for what they are, make a choice to be happy and then consciously co-create to bring about change. Meditation brings about change in the quickest of ways. For those who are not into meditation, it's understandable. However, it is very beneficial to the ego taming process. The act of quieting your mind creates a pause between what's going on and your reaction. It does this naturally, without any conscious training.

Ego does not stand a chance because, in meditation, the soul connects with the spirit and grows stronger than the carnal mind. When you come out of meditation and go along with the activities of daily living changes will happen to your entire perspective of life. It creates a calmness where before was chaos.

Things that used to bother you don't anymore. Humans sift through all types of coping mechanisms to deal with pain and they don't realize they have a built-in analgesic.

Creating the gap in reaction will give you the ability to change your life. You are the painter and consciousness is the paint. Your life is the canvas and you can paint anything you wish. To go down a spiritual path is to unlearn what has been learned in order to create room for you to remember what you already know. The fastest way to remember is through meditation. Often enough, spiritual teachers emphasize the need to meditate. The concept is foreign to most people in a westernized cultural setting.

We have been taught to seek outside of ourselves for answers. Some eastern philosophies teach that meditation is the only way to spiritual enlightenment. Rules have exceptions and the same is true for spiritual practices. Meditation is not necessarily for everyone. Without it, it is like boarding a flight that has two long layovers and then circles the air for a while before landing. There were quicker flights, you just chose to take the long route.

Meditation is intimate time with the Creator. It is the seeking of God's "face" from the insight of the inside. Sitting in silence with yourself is no different than sitting in silence with Source. It is likened to receiving a response when the petition is the prayer. How can you ask for something if you don't shut up long enough to hear the answer? Sometimes you will receive a plan immediately and sometimes you won't, but if you listen long enough you will always get your answer.

Meditation allows truth to communicate with absolute truth. To understand oneself gives the seeker the ability to listen to his/her own intuition. The inner guide can get loud in certain instances, but mostly it is quiet and speaks in a whisper. In the midst of the gap of event and reaction, intuition acts like a guide. Meditation strengthens intuition. Your intuition will let you know that you are on the right track because you will have an inner confidence. You will just "know" things.

Meditation also teaches us about the dualistic nature of human beings. For example, when you sit down and meditate you will realize how autonomic random thoughts are. The brain is good for focusing on the very thing you don't want to focus on. Like right now, if I told you not to think about bananas... don't think about bananas. What would your brain do? Think about bananas. The more we try to ignore something, the more our brain screams at us to pay attention to it. So as soon as you tell yourself, "Ok, I am going to be quiet and meditate," what does the brain do? Start thinking about a million things at the same time. You start thinking about everything else when you are supposed to be quieting the mind. It's frustrating because you are telling yourself, "NO! Don't think about that! Stop thinking."

Most people try it out, go through this, and give up. They say, "I talk too much" or something like, "My brain just won't shut off. "This is just a wonderful example of how the brain and its thoughts and the conscious mind are two separate entities. As you sit there with your eyes closed and pay attention to these thoughts, you will begin to realize that YOU are paying attention to these thoughts. This is proof that you are not your thoughts. You are who what pays attention to these thoughts and they are going to come whether you want them to or not. In the beginning stages of meditation, mind clearing, silent contemplation or whatever you want to title it, we will all experience the chitter chatter of the autonomic mind. Any attempt to consciously ignore this inner dialogue will only result in more brain chatter. So, what is the solution? How do you discipline this stubborn and unruly brain?

The answer is you don't. You let it be but do not attach yourself to the process. Watch the thoughts come and go. Realize they are going to do that regardless of how bad you want them to stop because they are not you and you are not them. They are a possession. You have thoughts; you own thoughts; you are not thoughts. This is your formal introduction to the "witness."

There is a spiritual trait that usually doesn't get revealed until we are well into our spiritual journey. It is the aspect of the silent witness. The witness is the focal point of consciousness that is separate from the mind. It is the watcher. It is a part of consciousness but as we grow spiritually its partition becomes more apparent. This is another paradox; consciousness that is separate yet combined.

During meditation, you become aware of the sensation of being inside the body. You become more tuned in to the witness who lives inside of the body with you. You become aware of self. You may be able to feel sensations of the skin, blinking of the eyes, although the eyelids are closed. Your eyes are still open actually. They are just viewing the other side of your eyelids instead of the outside world. Meditation allows you to become detached from outside stimuli and in turn, allows spirit to become the puppet master of your essence.

Spirit will be in complete control of your possessions, including your thoughts. In the silence of the inner being, we are reunited with our original birthplace, the consciousness of God that was present before existence existed. Before the Big Bang of matter, there was this infinite consciousness that always was and always will be. Spiritualists call it "The Void." Meditation blocks out the five senses and merges us with the Void. In that moment, the mind of God and our mind are one.

In the silence, we experience moments of simplistic contemplation and then, there are moments of powerful divine revelation. There are moments of vivid images and there are moments of overwhelming emotions all found in that quiet. To be honest, meditation changes people for the better. There is a whole other world within your mind that is full of peace, energy, and beauty. You can feel God's love so deeply in this sweet abyss of silence because you are more open to receiving it.

There are methods available for those people are not experts at this and still are at the beginning stages. The easiest method is called The Watch Method. The goal of this is to capture the moments of random thoughts consciously, watch them, and accept them. That is, it. The mind is like a spoiled child. When you don't give it the attention it wants, eventually it will stop throwing a temper tantrum and get with the program. Another method is called the "Back to Basics" method. This is also an original technique that I developed for myself because my mind was so active at the very beginning of my meditation journey.

To do this: you can attempt to clear your mind and relax but remain conscious. When the autonomic thoughts pop up you do not try to get rid of them, you just distract yourself by refocusing your energy on your own breathing pattern. You perform rhythmic breathing until the thought goes away.

Still, another plan is called the "Bubble" method. This method uses visualization in the midst of meditation. When we are clearing our mind and the thoughts are coming into them we envision the thought becoming trapped in a bubble and the bubble floating up out of our mind. All we have to do is relax and watch the bubbles. Or we can visualize the thought as a drop out of the ocean that is the mind of the Source of All. Honestly, that is what it is anyway so what better thing to visualize? This will keep the bigger picture of reality in the forefront.

Just because the drop is separated from the ocean doesn't mean it not a part of the ocean. It came from the ocean, therefore, it will always be a part of the ocean. Likewise, we are not separate from God. We came from God; therefore, we will always be a part of God.

The "Exit Stage Left" technique visualizes the thought that intrudes on us like it is standing on a stage. Our form, visualized, walks the thought off the stage. You don't have to spend the entire time in meditation thoughtless. It's understood, already, that we don't have a lot of time in our busy schedules to spend doing absolutely nothing. Most of our lives are filled to the brim with activity and responsibility. Good thing, like everything else, meditation can evolve to fit into modern times. You just have to figure out which one fits best for you.

There are a number of forms of traditional techniques. For example, monks have a meditation where they are in meditation while walking. We can also use meditation while driving, believe it or not. Driving mediation is only to be used when the route being followed is well known to the driver and the person is fully experienced behind the wheel. You can use that time to consciously be thoughtless, be prayerful or even visualize. There is no such thing as being totally thoughtless while driving because you still need to retain some focus to drive but in that time, you can turn off the radio and calm your mind with some quietness.

All you need while seeking truth and desiring a better spiritual connection with Source is an open heart and an open mind. Remember, expectations are the enemy. Some people get it right away and all of this comes easy to them. Others take more time but we should each be happy and grateful for our life and our relationship with Source even if it never changes.

Negative thoughts are self-inflicted punishment. The Divine Spirit has endless love and compassion for each one of us regardless of how we live. The care of self is the act of being grateful for this fact. Leading a more spirit-filled life, learning spiritual knowledge, and growing spiritually can and will change our lives for the better. This is a 100% guarantee.

-Spiritual Junkie-

Something all spiritual teachers encourage is some form of routine to follow to keep one focused while dwelling in an urban society. Most of us use prayer or meditation, but there are other ways to cope as well. Affirmations are a good way to stay spiritually grounded. They are positive phrases that are either said aloud or in your head. They can either be borrowed from someone else or an original thought. Another name for them is mantras.

Mantras are conscious reminders of what we want to remember. On a more modern twist, they don't have to be deep or long or something you think someone else would say. You can personalize your mantras and do whatever feels comfortable for you. Most would agree that the morning time is the best time to practice a spiritual exercise to start the day off on a positive note.

Putting gratitude and desires into the atmosphere with good intentions will always yield good results. Prayers call desire into existence and make reality continue to expand. It is how we contact those who have been assigned to come to our aid. It is how we commune and converse with God.

Praying is well known, but visualization is less well-known. This is the act of using the imagination to pull visions from the thought world to the real world. There are hundreds of visualization techniques on the internet you can learn or you can make up your own. This is good for cleansing the body of negative vibes, getting rid of sickness, and focusing on goals. You can't do it if you can't see yourself doing it. People who are sensitive to other people's energies find protection visualizations very useful. You can do this at any-time and anywhere. There is no special set of techniques to follow.

Acupuncture, although it does not have scientific proof, has been known to help clear energy through the body. It is an ancient Chinese practice that focuses on the Qi or Life force energy. People use it for a number of things, from treating insomnia and physical ailments to helping them stop smoking. Western medicine is quick to scoff at its effectiveness but the truth is modern healthcare is set up to only trust its own standards. Western or modern medicine relies only on treatment protocols that it invented.

According to experienced Acupuncturist, Ronica Perez, the classical Chinese explanation is that Qi (Chee), an energetic substance, flows through our body in channels called meridians, just as blood flows through our veins. The Qi should be flowing harmoniously throughout the body but certain factors lead to this flow becoming disrupted. Factors that may lead to Qi not flowing properly include stress, over-taxation, or a poor diet to name a few. Pain, illness, or disease may result when the body is not in a state of balance.

The meridians can be influenced by needling the specific acupuncture points located in different parts of the body. The acupuncture needles unblock these obstructions and reestablish the regular flow through the meridians to restore the body to a state of balance. In a balanced state, the body is more able to resist invasions, heal from injuries, attain mental and emotional clarity, handle stress, and much more.

The modern scientific explanation is that needling the acupuncture points stimulates the nervous system to release chemicals in the muscles, spinal cord, and brain. These chemicals will either change the experience of pain, or they will trigger the release of other chemicals and hormones which influence the body's own internal regulating system.

EFT, is a more recent spiritual aid. It stands for Emotional Freedom Technique. It is a technique that removes emotional blockages from the spirit, mind, emotions, and body. It uses the same meridian points in the body that acupuncture uses. Some even call it spiritual acupuncture. An older technique that helps, but is not utilized nearly enough is hypnosis. Hypnosis unblocks and helps solves problems arising from the subconscious.

There are experts in the fields that perform some of the previously mentioned skills and you can find a class that will teach the average person how to do them themselves. YouTube has guided self-hypnosis videos and guided meditation videos. These are a few of the vast spiritual practices that are out there but the best advice to give is find the technique that works best for your individual soul's energy.

"The word yoga means skill, skill to live your life, to manage your mind, to deal with your emotions, to be with people, to be in love and no let that love turn into hatred."

Yoga uses the body to gain access to the spirit instead of using the mind as a middleman. It cleanses the deepest layers of consciousness through teaching and learning of proper relaxation and breathing techniques. It is mostly used in the westernized world for exercise but originally yoga was used strictly for spiritual reasons. Yoga means "joined together". It comes from the ancient Sanskrit root word *yug,* which means "to unify."

Reiki is a newer alternative treatment as well. It is done by practitioners to heal Qi energy. Reiki has the ability to diminish the pain body and dispel negative energy that has attached itself to our auras from past traumatic episodes. This can be used for raising vibrations although there is no scientific evidence that Reiki works. There is also no scientific evidence about Crystal use but there is a plethora of information about crystal properties and usage.

New age practitioners develop rituals where the goal is to balance mind, body, and spirit through crystal usage. It is the belief that the minerals engrained in crystals descend from live organisms. This unusual pairing results in vibrational benefits to the user or the wearer. Different crystals hold different properties and aid in raising vibrations during rituals. The internet has an abundance of information regarding ancient and more modern practices.

Mindfulness is a meditation in itself. This is conscious meditation. To be mindful means to be aware of our actions and our thoughts at all times and to just be an observer of them. It means paying attention to the present moment of our daily lives, in that moment, not just going through the motions of them. An example would be to observe how driving has become second nature to us after years of experience on the road. Driving is something we no longer think about. We just do it. We drive home and don't even remember the moves we made and the steps we took to get there. To be mindful would be to drive home and not think about anything else but driving home. Mindfulness lessens stress and declutters the brain. Stress comes from focusing on the past or focusing on the future. In this very present moment, there is nothing but peace.

Mindfulness is being present in each moment no matter how minor the moment. It is embracing all your moments without looking in the past or looking in the future. It is feeling the joy and feeling the pain and knowing it is all a part of the gift of life. It is embracing all the aspects of being. In order to be mindful all, you have to do is "be."

"Sleep is the best meditation," the Dalai Lama teaches. That sounds weird to say knowing there are hundreds of meditation techniques out there, but there is a good reason he says this. We live in a busy world and in order to keep up with it, most of the time we push our bodies to their physical limits. We exhaust our life force and usually don't even pay attention to the fact our bodies are screaming for rest. We think that this is what is required to be good workers, good parents, and even good spiritualists. This couldn't be farther from the truth. You cannot pour from a cup that is empty. Take care of yourself first. Relax, rest and get enough sleep. This will give you the energy to raise your vibrational levels.

Music can be used when there is no available time for quiet. Music is the purest form of vibration that we have available to us. YouTube is a good source to find music like Tibetan singing bowls, shaman drum sounds, soft flutes, and even rain sounds that we can meditate to or just relax into the soothing atmosphere. Kids and family life make it hard to find quiet time. You can use a phone with some earbuds, plug in, and tune out, even if it's just for five minutes. The idea is simply to provide balance to the "busy, busy, busy" of life.

We deal with huge amounts of mental stress on a daily basis in modern society and meditation will help to even us out. It soothes the weary and frazzled mind and even gives us a temporary mental vacation. Dancing and music are natural stress relievers and should be taken advantage of as often as possible. Create a library of go-to songs that make you feel good and/or think about good times. It doesn't have to be a specific genre, just pick the music that you like. When you feel down, turn that music up and sing your heart out. So, what if you can't really sing? Who cares if your kids are looking at you like you are a crazy person? Enjoy the moment. Make time to make enjoyable moments. Laugh as much as possible as often as possible. These listed subjects are all aides in our quests for spiritual freedom.

Surrounding yourself with good people and loving animals also help in tough times. Developing a spiritual regimen is very helpful as well. Above all, we have to remember who we really are and what we are really doing here. It is easy to forget. You don't just wake up one day and you're enlightened and all your problems are gone...unless you run away to a Tibetan Buddhist monastery, in the real world, you are going to have real-world problems. No matter what, if you know who you are, you know your real power and that makes roadblocks seem like potholes.

Opening up to different spiritual planes of growth will make life that much easier. As we continue to grow, life's mysteries will become clear. We have so many unanswered questions as a people. Where do crop circles come from? What does déjà vu mean? Did the ancient continents of Atlantis and Lemuria really exist? What happens during conception? What happens during the transition of death? What were we doing before being born? How do mediums and psychics get their gifts? Is Astral Projection real? Spirituality is a rabbit hole and it can go as deep as you want it to go. Just know that your expectations and your limits will limit your growth.

Attachment to old habits will keep suffering in the forefront. Instead of fighting against the current, just lay back, relax and go where the currents of life take you. Life is a journey, not a destination.

At the beginning of the spiritual path, in our quest to obtain truth, we sometimes gather our info at a rapid pace. As it slows down, our customized path will become clearer and clearer. Awareness removes the ego as boss of controlling day to day emotions. Thought processes will now be dominated by the spirit. The more we grow spiritually, the less the ego is in control. There are times when our energy is directly connected to the source without effort. By simply knowing who we are in relation to the Source of All that makes the spiritual bond even stronger. We begin to walk in our own truth while reserving judgment for truths that are different than ours. This is how you obtain and keep daily unwavering peace.

So many times, we get caught up in the clichés of being spiritual and acting spiritual, especially when we've tried a particular organized religion and it did not work. We feel our perspective shift and observe our vocabulary change with the increase of knowledge. Your outward appearance and activities may change as well but you have to be careful not to create or trap yourself into another belief system. Beliefs can change and evolve. Always remember that.

The desire to be accepted and admired may cause us to pretend like we understand something we not only don't understand but may not even be meant for our own particular spiritual journey. People pursuing spiritual paths are still people and still have to deal with their own egos and shortcomings. We will make mistakes, make bad choices, and hit bumps in the road like everyone else. It is important to remember that no matter how much spiritual knowledge aids your process, true peace and enlightenment comes from within, not without.

The outward seeking for another person or thing is essentially the cry for our true self and the part of us that was missing will start to return. The lonely feeling, we had at the beginning of the journey will disappear with time. Gradually a deeper peace will arrive and we will feel more complete and whole. We will enjoy spending time with ourselves because we will have become our own best friend.

And when we do spend time with our loved ones or friends it will be more natural and relaxed and less co-dependent. No longer will there be the puzzling neediness of trying to grab a piece of another to force fit it into the missing space of ourselves and all of the wheeling, dealing and stealing of psychic energy that goes with the attempt: "Well if you do this for me, I'll do this for you." "If you ignore this about me, I'll ignore this about you" etc. We won't have a dependence on others for acceptance. Finally, we are standing in our own truth and it is the best feeling ever.

You will notice when you are alone you are no longer lonely. In fact, you will feel like you are gathering more of yourself to yourself so that when you are in the company of others you will have more of yourself to share. Solitary time will be "soul-itary" time. Aloneness will be experienced as all-oneness.

Many religious groups and organizations have evolved over time through the marrying of spirituality and political correctness of a particular ideology of that particular era. True spirituality is the path of the mystic. It is the path of exploration through personal experience, without religious dogma and it is practiced in the laboratory of the soul. It is the path of recognition of Truth.

In the book, Anatomy of the Ego, author, Bhagwan Ra Afrika quotes the famous African proverb that says, "Know Thyself. Have your religion if you must but know yourself." Enlightenment is a level of deep spiritual understanding. You, now, understand the purpose of life and why things happen the way they happen. Life will never go smoothly at all times. There will be setbacks and pitfalls along the way but we know that everything happens for a reason.

We have more than belief at this point. We have knowing. Knowing self, puts our roles into a deeper perspective as they relate to universal principles. We learn that we must balance our own personal yin and yang in order to master our lives. Yin is the feminine principle everyone has inside. It is divine, gentle and focuses on earthly priorities. Yang is the masculine principle, it is a warrior, strong and harbors our masculine side.

Light warriors achieve enlightenment through the strength of their will. They understand spiritual principles such as self-love, self-acceptance, self-mastery and trusting the universe and themselves. They understand that their thoughts create their reality and wield the thoughts as mighty swords to awaken the consciousness within themselves and the planet. Spiritual knowledge awakens our inner spirit and benefits our life path.

Different paths intermingle and intersect and we tend to attract those who we've forged soul contracts with or have loved in previous existences. Not all the information we receive is going to resonate with those around us and that is ok. The spiritual path is about exploration and revelation. No two paths are the same. Spiritualists know how to season and stir their spiritual gumbo. The spoon is their open mind and heart.

After the wisdom has organized itself, it will fall into harmony with your own personal vibration. You will begin to not only know the material but live it as well. This time is exciting because the student is learning how to be the master. You are able to stand in your truth while accepting others who may not be able to relate or agree. You will be at peace with yourself regardless of what is going on around you.

Enlightenment is a process of opening up to a conscious state of being. Consciousness is an awareness of aspects of self and the act of looking at self as a spiritual entity. It allows our spiritual side to awaken from a state of automatic, autonomic, pre-programmed and unconscious behavior and thought patterns. The evolution of consciousness involves shifts of perception. At first, we are just functioning at a level of existence. We are doing whatever has been programmed for us to do according to our surroundings. Then, our thoughts expand to include more conscious thoughts. Our thoughts become more deliberate and purposeful.

We begin to think before we react. We gradually increase in self-awareness and self-love at our own designated pace. Age and maturity also contribute to this growth rate. Self-reflection leads to the unraveling of the ego from around the spirit. Analyzation of our lifestyle encourages change. We begin to pay attention to what we are paying attention to. We compare our thoughts to the thoughts of society as a whole and begin to take a spiritual inventory of what we agree with and what feels right to us.

There is more than one way to unlock the door to spiritual enlightenment. The path described in previous chapters details achieving spiritual enlightenment through left-brained acquirement of knowledge and letting it filter through the right-brained creative and emotional processes but there are many other ways that we can always seek and explore. Left brain applied spirituality is the study of spiritual material such as science, religion, philosophy, formulas, theories, numerology, mathematics and history studied in an analytical, logical and practical manner.

Right-brained applied spirituality is the study of spiritual material such as astrology, art, music, and nature among other things that are studied in an intuitive and imaginative way. Spiritual knowledge is not a learning of the "new," but it is a remembering of the old. We are ancient creatures. Our souls have been around for eons. This isn't our first rodeo at all.

If all else fails, unlocking your passion can also unlock nirvana. Follow your bliss in life. For example, some people have a passion for healthy living. They cherish and appreciate their physical bodies. They take a special concern to diet, exercise, and nutrition. By opening themselves up with self-love, the love grows into love for others and that love brings with it peace, joy, and a positive outlook on life.

Enlightenment can also be reached through self-discipline and denial. Fasting is denying oneself food or something else to pledge servitude to the Almighty Creator. The rejection of materialistic things allows for a more concentrated focus on the Most High and service to others. Gratitude always has an end result of joy, and joy will lead you to be at peace with yourself. Unconventional belief structures such as Wicca or utilizing psychic abilities can be a path to Nirvana, as well. The path is just an outward expression of an inward intention. Intention holds great spiritual power. It showcases the shift in perception from not just doing something to the reason why you are doing it.

Enlightenment is the awakening to your higher self which is God and God, of course, is love. Enlightened individuals function predominantly by their spirit mind and instead of their ego mind. Joy and inner peace are end products of reaching enlightenment. With reaching Nirvana, you will experience the bliss of merging with God. To be enlightened is to experience total freedom. Being able to navigate the physical world in a constant state of spiritual awareness is like being in the passenger seat of a car and not having to be the driver. You now know that the universe is in control and always has been in control.

There are no more power struggles for the steering wheel. You have gotten to the place of surrender. It is inevitable. With knowledge, comes responsibility. There is no point of seeking it if you don't apply what you've learned. Peace is not an outward notion that you are striving to find. You ARE peace and it is you. You ARE love and it is you. You forgot this but now, you are remembering.

Now that you are embracing life being the passenger instead of the driver, you will get to notice all kinds of details you couldn't fully pay attention to when you were busy driving. You get to stop and smell the roses. You get to appreciate the patterns the clouds make in the sky. You get to marvel at all of mankinds creations. You are able to expand your mind and enter any situation being at total peace with whatever outcome. You are no longer surviving, you are living and growing with every breath you take. Things that once bothered you do not bother you anymore because you know exactly who you are and where you are going.

You are a spiritual being in a physical body having an earthly experience for the sake of experience and growth. You are an aspect of the Creator experiencing itself from your focal point of consciousness. Knowing this gives you access to great power. Not only do you understand the game, you understand the rules. Your thoughts create your reality. You are no longer just a player in the stadium of life. You are the coach, the team and the audience in the bleachers. Your consciousness has expanded to embody the entire stadium. The coach is your soul, the players are aspects of your ego and the audience is your witness spirit. Your awareness is watching the game and the Universe/Creator is the stadium.

Your growth in discernment is more pronounced and sharpened. You will know what path is right for you no matter what everyone else around you is doing. Enlightenment can also be reached through religion, believe it or not. Some spiritual seekers disregard religion because of its rigid nature but service to the Creator can and will lead to joy and peace within. Faith is a jumpstart to enlightenment because it fortifies the beliefs of helping each other as God's children.

The human soul is capable of making good decisions regarding truth. Faith provides the drive to keep moving forward and growing despite our surroundings. Deities or religious holy figures are often examples of enlightened beings. They show us how to love unconditionally and give us an example of what peace looks like. Also, the salvation received through repentance and faith eliminates karma by the forgiveness of others and forgiveness of self. No matter which path we choose to get there, the path to enlightenment will increase our tolerance of other people's spiritual preferences.

We are all aspects of the Creator and we have been sent to this earth school to further our spiritual growth. Different people require different methods of teaching. When this is understood, it is respected.

We can now, go back to those big questions we asked before and begin to answer them. If we haven't gotten there yet, trust, it is coming. Just stay on the path. The paradox of God will always exist because the Creator doesn't prove its existence beyond a shadow of a doubt. This is to honor free will. We have the power to ignore the very consciousness that created our soul if we choose. Since the Source of All gave us that right, it is even ok to respect the opinions of those who deny the existence of the Supreme Consciousness.

We see the common paradox of people questioning how God can love us unconditionally, yet judge us, punish us and damn us at the same time with open eyes. Souls choose to come here prior to this incarnation. It fortifies soul contracts with loved ones who have agreed to aid us in learning our lessons. We assist in planning what obstacles we will face and what catalysts we will need for whatever spiritual principle we are going to work on when we get here.

We do not come here alone. We have aids in the form of our ancestors, our higher self, spirit guides and guardian angels. We have guardians who are assigned to us in the spirit world. If this is a test it would be defeating the purpose if God just handed over the answers. Some things have to run their course for the good of the lesson and we simply must go through it.

Even though we have made up different concepts regarding God, the true nature of God is unexplainable. It exists outside of the laws that govern us. All of our theories will still fall short of absolute truth because our own perception is limited. We only witness a tiny glimpse of what God actually is. This is why we have so many different definitions of God. Simply put, God is love, love is God and neither has any boundaries. The boxes we create in our own belief structures shrink God. We personify God and subject God to our own personality flaws and man-made rules. We cannot develop a completely accurate assumption of the Creator. There are things that will always remain a mystery.

We were birthed from the mind of God as individual units of consciousness to co-create in this ever-expanding universe. Love is our greatest and most powerful tool of co-creation. Expanding consciousness and seeking enlightenment is about expanding from conditional love to unconditional love. Conditional love has a limit and a boundary. It is love under the right circumstances; it is giving, as long as we are getting something back.

True love is service and selfless. It is a giving of one's self and seeking nothing in return. Unconditional love eliminates karma. Conditional love breeds karma. Love and gratitude grow the spirit and shrink the ego. Happiness is always a choice and there is always some form of choice no matter the situation. No matter the choice, we know all is a part of a divine plan.

There is no such thing as a mistake or an accident because every catalyst brings with it the opportunity to love, which is what we came here for in the first place. Love is like a muscle. The more you use it, the stronger it gets. Until it becomes second nature, it is easy to lose focus and slip back into old habits. Fortunately for us, we have developed certain techniques to keep us focused. Striving for enlightenment can have its ups and downs. Natural inspirations are not prominent all the time because of all the stressors of modern living. It's always good to keep our frequencies as high as possible. We can do this by ingesting things that are beneficial to the body, avoiding toxins, spending time in nature, and remembering to laugh as much as we can.

Everything you want to know to live a more spiritual life will be revealed to you by God-Source. It's not about the books you read, it's not about the seminars you attend; it is about your desire to know and your desire to be a better person. Have faith in the unseen forces that guide you and have faith in yourself. You are more powerful than you are even aware of. It's ok to walk in that power. It isn't a sign of ego, it's a sign of egoless-ness. While you are searching for enlightenment, the truth is, you are already there.

-In Conclusion-

In conclusion, know you are not who you thought you were. You are not your body. You are not your identity, or your thoughts or your emotions. You are consciousness created from Divine Consciousness. You were sent here to grow spiritually. You were given the illusion of your ego, which houses all of your roles and your unique soul imprint. Your ego helps you maneuver through the game. What are you going to do with this knowledge? Knowledge is power. This knowledge can help you break your cycle of suffering.

"Spirituality is being conscious of reality."- Prof. James Small

"When we drop down from the ego into our heart, our souls will speak the truth."- Nancy Kerner

The first step to enlightenment and inner peace is to accept all things, whether they are good or bad. Acceptance eliminates suffering. Look past the "should be's," the viewpoints and the prejudices. The truth is that life IS what it is. Everything happens for a reason, even if we can't see the reason. Secondly, forgive those people and situations that may hold you back or have wronged you, even if you never get any closure. Forgive anyway.

Also, be sure to forgive yourself for any shortcomings you may have. This releases any negative karma you may have accumulated. Lastly, accept the fact that it is ok to be at peace. We don't have to suffer to reach enlightenment. We have other options. We don't have to stay miserable because everyone around us is miserable. The world will give you whatever you give it. Life is rough but life is, ultimately, what you make of it.

"Sometimes surrender means giving up trying to understand and becoming comfortable with not knowing."- Eckhart Tolle

"When I try to make things the way I would like them to be, I lose my inner peace and happiness. When I accept things the way they are and work peacefully with what is so, happiness finds me and fills me...and things start to fall into place effortlessly." – Asha

One thing is for sure, you cannot grow spiritually and not expect your perception to change. Moving from ego to spirit will change your entire outlook on life. There is nothing you can do to prevent it. Enjoy the journey and don't let anyone tell you that you are selfish for wanting to cultivate and grow your own spirit. Some people will not like the fact that you are living in the light while they are still in darkness. They are not there yet, but they will get there eventually, even if it is not this lifetime. Their souls are ancient and infinite, just like yours. Just trust that you have a reason for being here, even if you do not know what the reason is. There is no such thing as an accident or a coincidence.

"Being a candle is not easy; in order to give light, one must first burn."- Rumi

"You cannot grow unless you are willing to change. You will never improve yourself if you cling to what used to be." – Leon Brown

"No man is free who is not master of himself."- Epictetus

You may look out into the world and see negativity and the effects of this negativity. It is true. It is there. We are hardwired for NAT, negative automatic thinking. What we think, manifests. It is neither a surprise nor a coincidence that the state of the world is the way it is. An extremely negative catalyst will eventually yield extremely positive results. People are looking out at the state of the world and are beginning to break free from the psychological and spiritual brainwashing that has been imposed on us. People like us are being born daily.

We are born with a desire to seek the truth. In doing so, we are breaking generational curses, becoming an example to the next generation, even reprogramming our own DNA. We are making a subtle impact on the world because as we raise our vibrations we are sending that positivity out into the environment. That ingenious impact will eventually transform into a major force, even if that event happens three to four generations down the line. All human souls will eventually level up out of the third dimensions into higher levels of consciousness as a soul group. This is our destined future as a people.

"Even glow-sticks have to be broken before they will shine."- Unknown

"God is not an engineer sitting on a throne designing everything. God is everything. God is infinite energy and what that energy does is God doing it. Looking for God is like the fish looking for water."- Stephen Boston

The next generation will look to us as an example, apply what we have learned and in turn, teach the generation behind them. Eventually, the world will not look the way it does now. This is all part of the grand design that was written long before our current moment in time. There are plenty of things that we have forgotten. It looks like we are discovering new concepts but all we are really doing is remembering what was forgotten.

"There is a Divine Purpose behind every person and event that has ever come into our lives."- Neale Donald Walsch

Meanwhile, back on an individual level of growth, you will be able to see progress more and more. You already have progressed. The fact that you have the interest of tracking down spiritual knowledge is tremendous progress. Trust you will, your gut and your instincts, at all times, because those are the conduits of communication from the Universe.

There are plenty of people who have just accepted their existence as a miserable one and have also accepted there is nothing they can do about it. Those people will try to convince you that you are no different than them. Don't believe that because you are different. You comprehend that even though we are all the same and come from the same source, some of us do not understand our God-given birthrights. You realize your own power.

"Absorb what is useful, discard what is not, add what is uniquely your own."- Bruce Lee

"Life is a school, where you learn to remember what your soul already knows." – Unknown

You can do whatever you want to do. The gift of choice is the greatest gift we own. That is an empowering feeling. We are empowered beings. This gift is a direct reflection of God's unconditional love for us. Our choices have a cause and effect. This is how we learn. This is how we grow.

"People may hate you for being different and not living by society's standards, but deep down, they wish they had the courage to do the same." – Author Unknown

"Follow your bliss and the universe will open doors for you."

- Joseph Campbell

When you live life unconsciously, you live under the impression that life is set up as one problem that gets solves and life moves on to the next problem. When you become conscious, you understand that the moments in between the problems are the ones that really matter. You live life in the moment instead of just waiting for the next problem to occur. You will begin to be able to walk around with a joy in your heart where there used to be pain, sadness, and suffering.

"Pain is inevitable. Suffering is optional." – Buddha

As your awareness strengthens so will your ability to stand in truth. It is very easy to sometimes forget that we are powerful spirits because when we look out into the world, we do not see a reflection of that. The more time you spend in the world, the easier it is to forget all the things you have learned. When you do not follow the majority, you will always be the minority. The disadvantage is you have to dig a little deeper to stay in your truth. It is very easy to feed into negativity.

Whatever you feed your mind grows so if you are surrounded by negativity, it becomes easier and easier to forget the positivity. Spiritual seekers have found that some sort of daily reminder will help stay on the path of peace and love. What works best is a personal decision. Prayers, mantras, meditation, books among other things will help aid in your quest for enlightenment.

"People take different roads seeking fulfillment and happiness. Just because they're not on your road does not mean they are lost." – Dalai Lama

"Other people might not understand your journey, that's ok – it's not them." - Kate Spencer

"Knowledge leads to awareness. Being aware allows you to make an empowered decision. Deciding for yourself is the passage way to enlightenment. Seek knowledge and use it wisely." – Jeannine Sanderson

Spiritual knowledge is like a muscle. The more you use it, the stronger it gets. Life is in a state of constant change anyway so why not have it change for the better? There are no drawbacks to walking an enlightened path, only benefits. The behavior of the people surrounding you will not bother you as much. You will be able to love those who do not mean you well. You will be able to stay at peace in the midst of a storm. You will know the difference between compassion and weakness and how to apply it. It will not take painful exposure to suffering to teach you to learn a lesson anymore. Most importantly, you will have a personal relationship with your Creator and it will clear answers to the questions most important to you.

"The quieter you become, the more you can hear."

– Ram Dass

We all originate from the source of God. We are all inter-connected. Separation is an illusion so we can focus on our souls' journeys. Self-love is just as important as loving others. Focusing on love is the ultimate aid to humanity. If you fill your heart with love before every situation there will be no such thing as making a mistake. Human relationships exist to produce love. We forget this when we forget we are made from love and originate from the original source of love. God is Love and we are by-products of the stuff. It's encoded in our DNA.

"The kingdom of heaven is within you, and whosoever shall know himself shall find it." – Egyptian Proverb

So now what? What happens after you supped up so much spiritual insight that your head is swimming? What do you do when you've meditated so much that you are the new poster child for inner peace? What's next?

"There are only two mistakes one can make along the road to truth; not going all the way and not starting." – Buddha

The spiritual journey is never-ending. There is always something new to learn. There is always room to grow.

"The truth you believe and cling to makes you unavailable to hear anything new." - Pema Chodron

"If you cannot find peace within yourself, you will never find it anywhere else." - Unknown

The answer is the future is whatever you want it to be. The journey doesn't have a stopping point, so it's potential is infinite. Once you know who you are and why are here, you can explore whatever you like. The spiritual journey is about experiencing the freedom to enjoy life, not just sitting around, sucking up oxygen, going through life and waiting to die. Pursuing peace of mind has projectable added bonuses. It helps all of humanity because when you tune into the love frequency of the Most High you cannot help but pay it forward. This is a natural reaction. You become a conduit and a conductor of love energy. As it flows through you, it flows outward as well.

"Happiness does not depend on what you have or who you are; it solely relies on what you think." – Buddha

"Experience life in all possible ways- good- bad, bittersweet, dark-light, summer- winter. Experience all the dualities. Don't be afraid of experience, because the more experience you have, the more mature you become."- Osho

That is it. That is all. There is nothing more to be said! You know the truth...well, the truth thus far. There is more to come. Go! Live! GROW! You can do this!

-Peace and Love, Aisha-

Index

Author's Bio

Aisha was born and raised in Chicago, Illinois and currently lives in the Chicago south suburbs with her tribe of miniature souls. She has a background in Christianity, including becoming a licensed Christian Minister, and has spent the last eight years following a non-structured spiritual path.

She has been studying religion, enlightenment, awareness, and metaphysics, extensively, since she was twenty years old.

Aisha has spent the past twenty years performing physical healings as a certified wound care nurse and mental/emotional healings as a Spiritual Counselor and Life Coach.

Index

Contact Information

Aisha Brackett

www.Urbanawakenings.org
Urbanawakenings1@gmail.com
Facebook: Aisha The Goddess Brackett
Facebook: Urban Awakenings
Twitter: @AishaThegoddess
LinkedIn: Aisha Brackett

Index

A

a, 5, vi, vii, 8, 9, 10, 11, 12, 13, 14, 15, 16,
17, 18, 19, 20, 21, 22, 23, 24, 25, 26,
27, 28, 29, 30, 31, 32, 33, 34, 35, 36,
37, 38, 39, 40, 41, 42, 43, 44, 45, 46,
47, 48, 49, 50, 51, 52, 53, 54, 55, 56,
57, 58, 59, 60, 61, 62, 63, 64, 65, 66,
67, 68, 69, 70, 71, 72, 73, 74, 75, 76,
77, 78, 79, 80, 81, 82, 83, 84, 85, 86,
87, 88, 89, 90, 91, 92, 93, 94, 95, 96,
97, 98, 99, 100, 101, 102, 103, 104,
105, 106, 107, 108, 109, 110, 111, 112,
113, 114, 115, 116, 117, 118, 119, 120,
121, 122, 123, 124, 125, 126, 127, 128,
129, 130, 131, 132, 133, 134, 136, 137,
138, 139, 140, 141, 142, 144

abandoned, 38, 92

absorbed, 34

acceptance, 13, 17, 20, 21, 69, 79, 85,
126, 127

Acupuncturist, 120

adolescence, 19

alarm, 14, 81

Aligning, 97

always, vi, 9, 18, 22, 28, 35, 49, 50, 71,
72, 79, 81, 84, 90, 92, 93, 95, 97, 109,
110, 114, 116, 117, 119, 128, 129, 130,
131, 132, 133, 139, 141

answer, 30, 41, 42, 45, 61, 64, 66, 75, 83,
105, 114, 115, 131, 142

anxiety, 14, 92, 106

attachment, 24, 26, 27, 81

attachments, 26, 27, 29

avenue, vii

aware, 15, 19, 20, 23, 35, 37, 38, 48, 56,
60, 61, 68, 79, 101, 109, 116, 122, 134,
140

awareness, 16, 30, 37, 38, 40, 46, 48, 51,
56, 57, 64, 80, 107, 108, 109, 128, 130,
131, 139, 140, 144

B

Becoming, 19

behavior, 13, 15, 21, 23, 35, 77, 78, 79,
106, 111, 112, 128, 140

behind, 38, 58, 61, 62, 76, 81, 94, 101,
102, 118, 137

beliefs, 8, 9, 15, 17, 18, 21, 24, 29, 33, 40,
54, 72, 84, 87, 93, 131

believe, 9, 11, 20, 23, 31, 34, 46, 47, 54,
72, 74, 84, 87, 90, 91, 96, 107, 111,
112, 118, 131, 138, 141

beneficial, 78, 113, 133

better, 19, 29, 31, 39, 40, 60, 63, 75, 78,
85, 91, 99, 102, 103, 106, 107, 108,
110, 116, 117, 118, 133, 140

birthrights, 138

bliss, 52, 64, 71, 97, 129, 139

bothers, 98

boundaries, 25, 33, 34, 73, 96, 132

brain, 14, 15, 24, 32, 34, 36, 48, 56, 80,
81, 93, 99, 111, 112, 114, 115, 120,
122, 128

broken, 10, 42, 65, 108, 137

C

cannot, vii, 11, 15, 23, 27, 34, 35, 39, 44,
46, 56, 62, 79, 80, 87, 96, 102, 105,
112, 123, 132, 135, 136, 141, 142

Index

Index

Index

Index

Index

www.ingramcontent.com/pod-product-compliance
Lightning Source LLC
LaVergne TN
LVHW021342080426
835508LV00020B/2075